NEEDLEWORK
ANTIQUE FLOWERS

NEEDLEWORK
ANTIQUE
FLOWERS

ELIZABETH BRADLEY

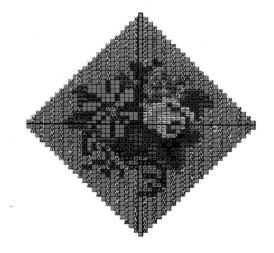

Photographs by Nadia Mackenzie

EBURY PRESS
LONDON

This book is for Emma, my editor, and for Colette
without whose help it would never have been finished in time.

MY THANKS TO NADIA MACKENZIE
and her assistant Chas Wilder
for the wonderfully accomplished, fresh and decorative photographs
which have great style and are such an essential and integral part of this book.

To Dafydd and Victoria Gruffudd Jones, Leonard and Dorothy
Ratcliffe and Robert and Josyane Young who allowed us to use
their houses in Beaumaris, Anglesey, Halstead, Essex and Battersea,
London as locations for the various photographs. Their kindness
and cooperation made each photographic shoot a pleasure.

My thanks also to all the needlemen and women who
stitched the models throughout this book and to Gillian Hughes who
organized their making. This book would have been quite
impossible to undertake without their help.

First published in 1993 in Great Britain by Ebury Press an imprint of Random House
Random House 20 Vauxhall Bridge Road London SW1V 2SA

3 5 7 9 10 8 6 4

Text and charts © Elizabeth Bradley 1993
Photographs © Nadia Mackenzie 1993
Photographs on pages 8–9 and 110–11 © Tim Imrie 1993
Sunflower border on pages 70-1 © The Rachel Kay-Shuttleworth Collection Trustees
at Gawthorpe Hall, Lancashire

British Library Cataloguing-in-Publication Data

A catalogue record for this book is available from the British Library.

ISBN 0 09 177122 6

Editor Emma Callery
Designer Janet James
Photographer Nadia Mackenzie
Assistant Chas Wilder
Stylist Elizabeth Bradley
Illustrator Isabelle Brent

Typeset in Goudy Old Style
by SX Composing Ltd, Rayleigh, Essex
Printed and bound in Italy by New Interlitho S.p.a., Milan

PREVIOUS PAGE: *The four seasons'
samplers, worked on linen, have been
framed and hung on a wall of mellow pine
panelling. On the window seat below, the
same four designs, worked in woolwork,
have been made into cushions.*

Contents

Introduction

ERANTHIS is an aconite
As everybody knows,
And HELLEBORUS NIGER is
Our friend the Christmas rose.
GALANTHUS is a snowdrop,
MATTHIOLA is a stock,
And CARDAMINE the meadow ·
flower
Which you call lady's smock.
MUSCARI is grape hyacinth,
DIANTHUS is a pink –
And that's as much as one
small head
Can carry, I should think.

"Those Latin Names", *Green Fingers*,
Reginald Arkell

This book has been a pleasure to write as it involves two of my major interests and pursuits, needlework and gardening. Needlework has been both a personal pastime and also my career for many years, it started with the buying and selling of period needlework and continues with the designing and painting of embroidery charts for other enthusiasts to work from. The old led to the new and even now my designs show the strong influence of antique pieces seen or bought over the years. The time spent looking around the shops and auction rooms of Britain trying to find particularly exquisite pieces of period needlework was not only fun but also the perfect training ground for any designer with a penchant for antique style.

Gardening, however, has never been anything but a very interesting and satisfying hobby: healthy when I am outside engaged in its actual practice and relaxing when inside reading gardening books and planning for the future. In fact, I often read gardening books in bed at night as I find that the trials, tribulations and successes of gardeners past and present however riveting at other times of the day, are extremely soporific at night. My tired mind is filled with idyllic pictures and good resolutions which happily I am unable to to anything about lying in bed.

One of the nicest things about writing this book was all the horticultural reading that was suddenly not only justifiable but totally necessary. Wading through endless volumes of poetry and plays looking for suitable snippets and quotes was also very enjoyable. Herbals too, made fascinating reading. These early plant manuals are a mixture of cookery book, medical text book and encyclopaedia of plant lore and legend. Gerard's *Herbal* came out as the clear favourite and you will find several of his succinct descriptions throughout this book.

Many of the earliest gardening books are surprisingly sophisticated. Roman gardeners such as Virgil and Pliny appear to have felt much the same about their plants as do modern gardeners. It sometimes seems to me that the only major changes in the last thousand years are the number of species and varieties of a particular genus that we now grow and the number of foreign plants that have been imported over the centuries.

"I'd sing perhaps of rich gardens, their planning
and cultivation,
The rose beds of Paestum that blossom twice
in a year,
The way endive rejoices to drink from a rivulet,
The bank all green with celery, the
cucumber snaking
Amid the grass and swelling to greatness:
I'd not forget
Late-flowering narcissus or gum arabic's
ringlet shoots,
Pale ivy, shore loving myrtle . . .

His the first rose of spring, the earliest apples
in autumn:
And when grim winter still was splitting the
rocks with cold
And holding the watercourses with curb
of ice, already
That man would be cutting his soft-haired
hyacinths, complaining
Of summer's backwardness and the west winds
slow to come.
His bees were the first to breed,
Enriching him with huge swarms: he squeezed
the frothy honey
Before anyone else from the combs: he had limes
and a wealth of pine trees:
And all the early blossom, that clothed his
trees with promise . . ."

The Georgics, Virgil (70-19BC)

Classic and Florists' Flowers

Another point that emerges from extensive garden reading is the cult of "classic plants" that have been grown in western gardens for a thousand years. Plants such as lilies, roses, pinks and violets have been extolled in poems and prose by generations of writers. They all have a whole collection of lore, legend and symbolism associated with them and are held in great affection by most gardeners. Many of these classic flowers also became florists' flowers whose history is one of obsession and devotion to a single genus. Individual species of this genus were improved and developed to such an extreme degree that the resulting plants were sometimes virtually useless for growing in the garden and had to be kept like delicate and rare pets in a special, protected environment. Auriculas, polyanthus, hyacinths, anemones, ranunculus, tulips, pinks and carnations were the original eight florists' flowers with violas, dahlias and chrysanthemums added to their ranks in the nineteenth century.

Modern gardeners and gardening writers seem to fall loosely into two schools. The first are plantsmen whom I greatly admire. They really know their charges, can remember their Latin names however often they change, and thoroughly understand what each plant needs to thrive. Their gardens, although often beautifully designed and laid out, differ from others by their plants also growing perfectly, each well staked and with enough space around it so that it can grow properly and be seen to best advantage. They know all the best varieties. They are professionals, patient, gentle and careful who find out what they should be doing and then carry it out to the letter.

I, as a gardener, fall into a second category that can only be described as the school of enthusiastic amateurs. I love my plants and know most of their names but just will not make the time to really find out what is necessary to get the best out of each. I am so eager to see what new plants will look like in place that I tend to stuff them into hastily-dug holes with a dash of bonemeal and hope for the best. Sometimes, of course, they grow splendidly but often it is a case of "could do better". My other problem is what almost amounts to a bare earth aversion. I like every inch of my soil from late spring to the first frosts to have a total covering of different degrees of green. Needless to say, under all this verdant and flourishing leaf, a certain amount of survival of the fittest is bound to take place. The casualties are often those rarities that I was so delighted to acquire only a few weeks or months before.

"Advice to a Young Gard'ner, On Planting and Rural Ornament

But before the young planter puts his foot upon the spade, we beg leave to caution him, in the strongest terms, against a want of spirit in Planting.

A slovenly Planter ranks among the most extravagant order of slovens: the labour, the plants, and the ground are thrown away, besides the consequent disgrace, not only to the individual, but to the Art itself."

Advice to Young Gardeners
Charles Marshall (1808)

This is basically a book about flowers, plants, gardens and needlework which includes a variety of floral designs which I hope you will enjoy working. It is not a book on how to garden, nor is it a herbal or a tome on garden lore or poetry. It does, however, contain a mixture of all of these and everything else that I find interesting about the particular flowers featured in the designs. It is written by an enthusiastic but amateur gardener who does not pretend to have nearly as much knowledge as she would like and probably not nearly as much as many of her readers.

OVERLEAF: *Hats being trimmed with bright summer flowers. A carpet, pictures and cushions all made from the Botanical Garden Series of flower designs complete the picture. The charts for The Lily, The Pansy and The Cyclamen from this series are on pages 58, 113 and 150.*

The History of Flowers in Needlework

Gardening is an ephemeral art, the work of one generation of devoted gardeners can be destroyed by the next who want to do something totally different with a particular patch of ground. Continuity is preserved only in a few famous gardens that are kept intact, or in forgotten gardens that are tucked away in remote places so that they escape the ravages of gardening trends. The fleeting pleasures and moments of satisfaction of gardeners through the centuries are often caught, however, in poetry and prose, in illustrations and in paintings. Incidents from the constantly changing procession of garden fashion are also immortalized in pieces of embroidery.

Floral embroidery has existed for as long as man has made gardens and gardeners have cultivated them. The flowers depicted in floral embroidery are usually very much the same as those most popular in gardens at the time when a particular piece of work was being sewn. Gardening trends thus played a large part in the selection of which bloom to stitch, though other factors such as the degree of beauty of a flower and its symbolic meaning were no doubt taken into consideration. In Tudor times, women from the more leisured classes were well versed in the classics and would have been well aware of the allegorical messages associated with the flowers that they grew and embroidered. Even the insects stitched among the flowers on early pieces of needlework had their meanings; snails stood for laziness, bees for diligence and moths for the transitory nature of human life.

Flowers in Early Needlework

Although plants and gardens were a passion in Tudor Britain, flowers were not popular as subjects for embroidery until after the Reformation. When the monasteries had been dissolved, fewer ecclesiastical pieces were needed and the attention of both professional and amateur embroiderers could turn towards more secular and frivolous themes; these included flowers.

> "What greater delight is there than to behold the earth apparelled with plants, as with a robe of embroidered works, set with orient pearles and garnished with great diversitie of rare and costly jewels."
>
> Gerard's *Herbal* (1597)

Sixteenth- and seventeenth-century clothes were lavishly decorated with gaily coloured plants and flowers worked in fine floss silks. House furnishings too were often embroidered with blossoms especially cushions, bed curtains and valances. Large, floral, stitched panels covered walls and flowery table covers were used to cover the long oak tables.

Sources and Trends of Flower Embroidery

Pieces of Tudor and Stuart floral embroidery often show a remarkable similarity, which indicates the use of pattern books as the origin of many of the designs. Several books of embroidery patterns were specifically printed for amateurs to work from at the end of the sixteenth and the beginning of the seventeenth century. The plant illustrations found in herbals also made good embroidery patterns as pages pricked with pins and discoloured with charcoal powder show.

Just as garden design changed with the times, so did the form of plants and flowers in embroidery. Changes only happened gradually so that unless a piece of work was dated or can be traced in an inventory or will, dating can only be approximate.

In Tudor and Stuart times, embroidered flowers tended to be highly stylized and formal whereas by the early eighteenth century, influenced by all things Indian and Chinese, foliage and blooms became increasingly whimsical and exotic. Formality was restored in about 1730 with stylized plants now arranged stiffly in urns, baskets and Delpht pots. Pieces of woolwork sewn in this style made very hard wearing and attractive carpets, covers for chairs and stools, and centrepieces for fire-screens.

Fifty years on, fashion once more changed and decreed realism to be the new trend. In the late eighteenth century, pretty and delicate blooms

> "Flowers, Plants, and Fishes,
> Beasts, Birds, Flyes, and Bees,
> Hil[l]s, Dales, Plaines, Pastures,
> Skies, Seas, Rivers, Trees;
> There's nothing neare at hand, or farthest sought,
> But with the Needle may be shap'd and wrought."
>
> *The Needle's Excellency* (1631)

"Could Time, his flight reversed
restore the hours
When, playing with they vestures
tissued flowers
The violets, the pink, the
jessamin
I pricke'd them into paper with a
pin."

On receipt of My Mother's picture
William Cowper

were worked in pastel-coloured silks on cream silken backgrounds, the individual flowers were often gathered together into charming posies tied with pale blue ribbons.

Victorian Embroidered Flowers

The nineteenth century brought Berlin woolwork, a totally new type of embroidery which was worked from charts produced in Berlin during the early years of the century. The designs on these detailed and fully coloured charts resembled tiny hand-painted mosaics; they were painted on to paper that had already been printed with a grid in a scale of 20 squares to the inch. Berlin woolwork soon became a craze and the new patterns were followed with enthusiasm by everyone from the Queen to middle-class ladies who aspired to gentility. Berlin charts were easy to follow and interesting to work and the results were colourful and attractive. The new Berlin wools were brilliantly coloured with aniline dyes and used with specially woven double canvas gave the work its highly characteristic appearance, cross stitch was the stitch most often used and it is the same stitch that is recommended for working the designs in this book.

The best Berlin woolwork flower designs were produced in the first 50 years of the century, after this date they became much clumsier and less desirable. They feature classic flowers like roses, violets, wallflowers, cornflowers, pansies, tulips, pinks and lilies plus many others that were new

and fashionable at that time. Oriental poppies, camellias, clematis, waterlilies and tender species such as datura and pelargoniums are all mixed together in elaborate bouquets, swags and wreaths.

The Influences of Eighteenth-century Embroidery

The designs in this book have been greatly affected by my fondness for both the formality of early needlework and the elegance of much eighteenth-century embroidery. Victorian woolwork charts and finished pieces have also been a major influence and a great source of interest for many years: their robust and colourful style is endlessly fascinating.

To these basic mentors add the charm of period flower portraits and the discipline of the illustrations found in early herbals. Most lately, the books of botanical engravings, sometimes called floralegia, which were produced in the eighteenth and nineteenth centuries have proved a great source of inspiration to me. Characteristic details from their pages such as butterflies and bees and the name of the flower written in one corner of each picture can be seen on several of the charts in this book – namely The Cyclamen, The Lily, The Pansy, The Iris and The Christmas Rose. Flower designs in whatever style or persuasion are great fun to work, the colours of the petals are so pretty and the shapes of leaves, buds and flowers so varied, that they lend themselves perfectly to having their portraits stitched in woolwork.

SPRING

SPRING

... What is Spring?
Growth in every thing –
Flesh and fleece, fur and feather,
Grass and greenworld all together;
Star-eyed strawberry-breasted
Throstle above her nested
Cluster of bugle blue eggs thin
Forms and warms the life within;
And bird and blossom swell
In sod or sheath or shell.
All things rising, all things
sizing ...

"The May Magnificat", Gerard
Manley Hopkins (1844-89)

Spring is an exciting time in the garden, by the end of winter the stiff points of bulbs are standing well up above the soil like groups of small spears, green and promising. The earth between them is bare this early in spring and I find it difficult to restrain myself from poking about in these apparently empty patches to see if this or that favourite plant has survived. Having damaged many precious plants in this way, I have learnt to leave them alone. If something must be done to help spring on its way, other than sitting by the fire and looking at seed catalogues, a spot of mulching is one answer. The spreading of a nice thick layer of nutritious insulation over the garden can be very satisfying.

"And in the springtime earth did put on her new cloathes, though had some cunning Herald beheld the same, he would have condemned her Coate to have been of no antient bearing, it was so overcharged with a variety of Colours. For there was yellow Marigolds, Wallflowers, Auriculusses, Gold Knobs, and abundance of other namelesse Flowers. There was White, the Dayes Eye, white roses, Lillyes, ... Violet, Irisse, Red Roses, Pionies ... The whole field was a vert of greene, and all the colours were present save sable, as too sad and dolefull for so merry a meeting."

Antheologia or The Speech of Flowers
Thomas Fuller (1660)

By the first day of spring, snowdrops – "Winters's timid child" who "awakes to life bedewed with tears" (Mrs Robinson, from *The Language of Flowers*) – have almost finished flowering and it is the turn of the crocuses to shine in the garden. The delicate species crocuses with flowers like stars which come from Turkey and Asia Minor flower especially early. *Crocus vernus*, the Dutch crocus, is the true spring flowering crocus, it flowers early on and has been grown in our gardens for over 300 years. This variety, so beloved of park gardeners, comes in various shades of purple, white, cream, purple and white stripes, and a rather virulent shade of orange.

I can live without this particular orange though on the whole I enjoy the bright colours of early spring flowers. At other times of the year, these brilliant hues might jar but after the long dark winter they are very welcome. Perhaps I notice such niceties less at this time of year because the little clumps of bulbs tend to be set well apart from one another in my garden. Each can be appreciated separately and their flowers are enhanced by the neutral brown of the earth around them.

As the season progresses I seem to get fussier and fussier and want rarer varieties and more subtle colours. Daffodils in particular need to be chosen carefully. They are such big, healthy bulbs and will grow almost anywhere, so one might as well have only the varieties that really appeal. My favourites are the white "Vigil" and the pale salmon and white "Rufford", both modern hybrids.

Spring is the time of year when I feel that I need a wood to plant rather than my small garden, for it would be nice to be able to plan in drifts rather than corners. There are so many bulbs I would like to grow but they would fill the available space in no time at all and then there would be no room for anything else. Room must be found for just a few more varieties, however. One that I would not be without is the tall and stately Easter lily, that smells of foxes. Its other name, Crown Imperial or *Fritillaria imperialis*, suits such a grand lady perfectly. Another variety well worth growing is the strangely checkered, snakeshead fritillary that

---

PREVIOUS PAGE: *Spring flowers spill out from a bag made from the Bunch of Spring Flowers design on page 45. Spring flowers make very pretty posies and the flowers on this table have been collected to make a selection of such small bunches or nosegays. The handle of the bag is made from the border pattern on page 46.*

looks delicate but it in fact grows like the proverbial weed. They are such rare and historic looking flowers that being able to grow them fills me with a quite unreasonable pride.

> "Let us now come and furnish the inward beds with those fine flowers that are most beseeming it: and namely Daffodils, Fritillaries, Jacinths, Saffron flowers, Lillies, Flower-de-luces, Tulipas, Anemone, French Cowslips or Beares eares, and a number of other such flowers, very beautiful, delightful, and pleasant, whereof although many have little sweete scent to recommend them, yet their earliness and exceeding varietie doth so farre countervaile that defect."
>
> *Paradisi in Sole Paradisus Terrestris,*
> John Parkinson (1629)

It would be sad to be totally without tulips in a garden, especially as they once turned normally sane gardeners into absolute fanatics. This was in the seventeenth century when tulipomania swept Holland and whole fortunes were won and lost on a single bulb. There are some modern cultivars that resemble the flamed, feathered and striped tulips from that period but seem to grow more satisfactorily. Two favourites of mine are "Van der Neer" which is a lovely tulip flamed in carmine and white and "Firebird", a handsome peach and green parrot tulip.

Space should also be found for a selection from the Primula family. The simple pale yellow, native primrose is hard to beat but for any antique plant lover, laced polyanthus and the fleshy leaved auriculas, or bear's ears, are very tempting. Many varieties can only be grown in pots but several of the border auriculas will grow into large clumps in a flower bed. I am inordinately proud of mine and their bold shape and colours make me want to reach for a paintbrush every year when they flower.

It is not surprising that auriculas were featured in so many old flower paintings and embroideries. The enormous diversity in the colour and form of the auricula is expressed in the poem by Reverend Samuel Gilbert from *Florist's Vade Mecum*:

> See how the Bear's Ears in their several dresses,
>   That yet no Poet's pen so high expresses,
>   Each head adorned with such rich attire,
>   Which Fools and Clowns may slight, whilst skill'd admire,
> Their gold, their purple, scarlets, crimson dies,
>   Their dark and lighter hair'd diversities,
>   With all their pretty shades and Ornaments,
> Their parti-coloured coats and pleasing scents,
>   Gold laid on scarlet, silver on the blue,
>   With sparkling eyes to take the eyes of you,
> Mixt colours, many more to please that sense,
>   Others with rich and great magnificence;
>   In double Ruffs, with gold and silver laced,
>   On purple crimson, and so neatly placed.
> Ransack Flora's Wardrobes, none sure can bring
>   More taking Ornaments t'adorn the spring.

In late spring, the first exciting shoots of herbaceous plants start coming through the earth, all fresh, bright and lime green in colour. Early perennials, like bleeding hearts, begin to flower next to the yellow daisies of doronicum and the pasque flowers, and wind anemones bloom and fill in the spaces. It is at this time of year that I am really glad that I took the trouble to plant all those long, heel cuttings of Bowles mauve wallflowers in last autumn's gaps. By mid-spring, these splendid plants are already bushing out and flowering profusely and by summer they will be huge.

When spring is nearly over, the roses begin to shoot and the greenfly really get into their stride in my studio garden. The snails leave the crannies in the stone walls and start to get their teeth into the new shoots of the hostas and dahlias. I know then that spring is at its end and summer is on its way.

The Spring Sampler

Here in a quiet and dusty room
they lie,
Faded as a crumbled stone or
shifting sand,
Forlorn as ashes, shrivelled,
scentless, dry –
Meadows and gardens running
through my hand.
In this brown husk a dale of
hawthorn dreams,
A cedar in this narrow cell
is thrust,
That will drink deeply of a
century's streams,
These lilies shall make summer on
my dust.

Here in their safe and simple
house of death,
Sealed in their shells a million
roses leap;
Here I can blow a garden
with my breath,
And in my hand a forest
lies asleep.

"The Seed Shop", Muriel Stuart

A seasonal sampler makes an interesting introduction to each of the four sections of this needlework book. The chart on page 19 is an attempt to design a pattern that would work both as a woolwork design and as a sampler plan. The woolwork piece could be worked, as usual, in tapestry wools on canvas and would make either a cushion or a picture. The sampler should be sewn in the traditional way with silks or fine crewel wool on unbleached linen. Cross stitch should be used for both pieces. The finished series of four seasonal samplers would make an unusual and decorative set of pictures as featured on page 2.

The theory and intention behind woolwork and sampler design are very different. In the eighteenth- and nineteenth-century historical style that I favour, woolwork design is both naturalistic and realistic. On the other hand, sampler design is much more formal and stylized. Images are normally flat and simple, representative rather than realistic.

Woolwork Design

By using different shades of wool like paint, an almost three-dimensional image can be built up in woolwork. A design does not have to be symmetrical but it looks best if both halves are reasonably balanced. The spaces between the various bits of pattern are very important and there must be enough of them or the picture will become confused and muddled. Carefully positioned spaces between elements of the design, such as leaves or buds, help to define their shape.

Just how interesting and attractive a piece of woolwork turns out to be depends on the colour, design and the degree of appeal of the subject matter. To a certain extent, these factors depend on the eye of the beholder, but in general pretty colours and subjects such as roses or kittens appeal more than, say, a beetroot or a three-toed sloth.

Woolwork was normally worked by adults, and its primary function is and has always been the decoration of the person or the home. For most people, the relaxation and satisfaction enjoyed while stitching, though very important as an incentive, is secondary to the decorative value of the finished piece.

Sampler Design

Samplers, however, came about for quite a different purpose. First known as examplers because they showed examples of different patterns and alphabets worked in rows down their length, they were in effect teaching pieces and needlework books all rolled into one. Samplers were normally worked by children and that they were pretty or charming, as well as useful, was purely incidental and brought about by the natural human desire to do a job well and to make the finished result as attractive as possible. It was only when a child or governess with some originality or creativity came along that samplers of particular charm were created.

Classic sampler design is almost invariably two-dimensional; the pictures and little motifs rely on representational traditions that were repeated over and over again for more than 300 years. Typically, they have a narrow border around the edge and bands of alphabets and small patterns and pictures filling the rest of the space. If a larger picture is present, such as a house or church, it is usually placed towards the bottom of the piece. The only samplers that really broke away from such rigid traditions were those worked in America during the late eighteenth and early nineteenth centuries. These tended to be worked in a mixture of stitches rather than just cross stitch and are both original and delightful. They feature wide flowery borders with bold, rather primitive, pictures in the centre. These often show people, animals, houses and

Each one of the four samplers in this book is surrounded by a frame of seasonal flowers. This spring flower frame includes violets, Lenten roses, primroses, aconites, heartsease, ranunculus, anenomes, leucojum, pasque flowers, polyanthus, muscari, fritillaries, auriculas and small daffodils.

Wool colours and quantities

The quantities listed below are the numbers of yards of Elizabeth Bradley Wool needed to work a piece measuring 169 stitches by 169 stitches on 10 mesh interlock canvas using cross stitch.

Colours used:
16 plus 1 background colour.

When working the woolwork on the right from the chart opposite, the red line border was omitted and four extra rows of background colour were worked around the edges.

The background colour used in the piece shown on page 2 is black (G11).

Number on Chart key	Elizabeth Bradley Wool colour	Quantity (yards)
1	B5	25
2	B7	30
3	C1	7
4	D2	18
5	D4	16
6	F8	8
7	F11	41
8	H3	11
9	I1	37
10	I4	40
11	I7	42
12	K5	42
13	J9	33
14	M10	17
15	N11	18
16	N10	12

Background quantity for a piece measuring 169 stitches by 169 stitches: 230 yards.

schools. Farms and gardens occasionally appear and even events from the small embroiderer's life such as weddings or outings are sometimes depicted in charming detail.

Combining a Sampler and Woolwork Design

Not surprisingly, combining the two strong design traditions of woolwork and samplers had its difficulties, but – after a certain amount of trial and error – the sampler charts on pages 19, 55, 91 and 130 were completed. The Spring Sampler features a formal and rather idealized vegetable garden in early spring. There is a minimal amount of shading on some of the flowers and garden objects but otherwise the design is two-dimensional. The colours of the wools and silks were selected to emphasize the seasonal nature of each sampler and so for spring a mixture of fresh spring greens, yellows, orange and purple were chosen.

Around the outside of the sampler there is a mixed border of purple violets and pale yellow,

1   2   3   4   5   6   7   8   9   10   11   12   13   14   15   16

Silk colours and quantities

The quantities listed below are the number of skeins of DMC six stranded perle cotton needed to work a sampler 163 stitches by 163 stitches. Each length of cotton should be split in half and the sampler worked with three strands only.

The sampler shown on page 17 was worked on 100% linen scrim, 91cms wide, which has approximately 20 threads to the inch. Each stitch should be worked over two threads.

Number on Chart key	DMC thread number	Number of skeins
1	356	2
2	355	2-3
3	ecru	1
4	677	1
5	834	1
6	640	1
7	3031	2
8	647	1
9	471	3-4
10	580	5
11	936	1
12	3363	2-3
13	890	2-3
14	3740	1
15	3041	1
16	3042	1

cream and rusty red primroses. In the centre it is, of course, raining: this is after all a British spring. At the top, there is a smart shed for tools, and a green painted trellis is fronted by a row of tulips and rabbits. Two robins sit on posts waiting for worms to be dug up for them to eat.

The beds below the top vignette are edged traditionally with box, in the manner of Tudor knot gardens. This sort of formal vegetable plot has survived to become part of the archetypal, walled, country house vegetable garden such as the one immortalized in the children's book *Peter Rabbit* by Beatrix Potter. The same tradition exists in old French vegetable gardens and was taken to America by the pioneers. On this sampler, some of the tilled and weed-free, box edged compartments are filled with tiny seedlings that have just "come up". Others hold young plants and unnaturally neat cauliflower and broccoli plants. One compartment is still bare and the central three hold violas, pink primroses and daffodils to give some spring colour.

On the lowest section of the sampler, a selection of garden equipment can be seen. A watering can and a seed tray complete with seedlings and terra-cotta pots full of tulips and daffodils are on one side while on the other there is a rhubarb forcer, a trug of vegetables with the handle of a trowel showing above its edge and another clay pot, this one containing Easter lilies. In the centre, there is a very neatly clipped holly bush still bearing its winter berries.

"You may mingle roots in their planting, many of divers sorts together, that they may give the more glorious show when they are in flower . . . Thus: the vernal crocus or saffron flowers of the spring, white, purple, yellow and striped, with some vernal colchicum or meadow saffron among them; some Dens Canis or dog's-teeth, and some of the small early leucojum or bulbous violet, all planted in some proportion as near one to another as is fit for them, will give such grace to the garden, that the place will seem like a piece of tapestry of many glorious colours, to increase every one's delight."

A description of how to use plants in the compartments of knot gardens from *Paradisi in Sole Paradisus Terrestris*, John Parkinson (1629)

Some of the capital letters from this alphabet can be seen in the names of the seasons on the samplers that begin each section of this book. I wanted a rather square and formal alphabet and this one seemed very suitable; it comes from a small nineteenth-century pattern book. I used a particularly square form of the capital M and W on the samplers as seen on the upper chart. A more conventional M and W can be seen on their own at the end of the lower chart. Finished pieces made from these two small charts can be seen on pages 124-5.

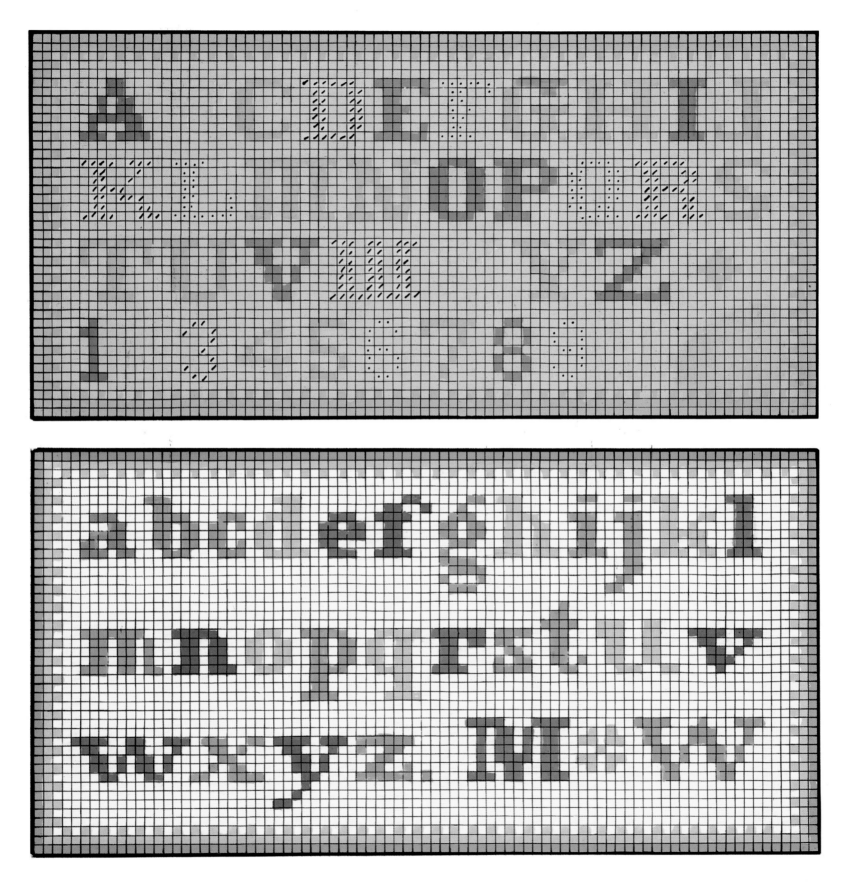

SPRING

The Blackbirds' Nest

"A creature that will destroy a song-bird's nest is a pest, and whether furred, feathered, four-legged, or a boy, ought to be exterminated."

Dr Abbott

Birds are as much a part of a garden as are the flowers growing in it, for the gardener and the birds it is a mutually rewarding relationship. The birds benefit from the seeds, insects and worms that they find there and are encouraged to nest by the ready availability of nesting sites in trees and shrubs. Some gardeners provide nesting boxes, a birdbath and food laid out on a birdtable as an added attraction. Marauding domestic cats are really the only black spot in an otherwise perfect bird environment. For their part the birds give the gardener endless pleasure with their songs, interesting behaviour and charm whether they are catching food, collecting material for their nests or feeding their infants.

Blackbirds are one of the stars of the garden, they sing melodiously and persistently with a rich warbling song punctuated by short pauses. The adult male blackbird is an impressive medium sized bird, about ten inches long with rich glossy black plumage, a bright yellow ring around the eye and an orange bill. The female and young birds are smaller and their feathers are a duller dark brown in colour with speckled breast feathers and a dark bill. They eat a mixed diet of seeds, fruit, insects and worms and the sight of a blackbird, head cocked to one side, listening for worms on the lawn is a characteristic sight in the early morning. Blackbirds are territorial and so unless a garden is extensive blackbirds may ration themselves to one family per garden.

Gardens are full of suitable nesting sites for blackbirds who like to build their nests well hidden in small trees, bushes or buildings. Generally the female builds the nest which is a well constructed affair of twigs and rootlets, lined with mud and completed with a soft layer of dried grass and moss. Three to five greenish-brown, speckled eggs are laid from March to August and incubation takes thirteen days. Both parents help to feed the young and each pair can raise from one to five broods each year.

Honeysuckle and Camellias

The blackbird nest in my design is sited amongst the soft yellow flowers of honeysuckle and the glossy leaves and waxy flowers of a camellia. Honeysuckle – or woodbine – grows wild in the hedgerows of Britain although the variety shown in this design, *Lonicera tellmanniana*, came originally from Budapest. It flowers in May and June and though it is not one of the most rampant varieties it will entwine itself through almost any shrub if allowed to do so. Its fresh green, rounded leaves and yellow or orange trumpet shaped flowers would certainly help to hide a nest and give the vulnerable nestlings extra protection.

Camellias originate from the mountains of Japan and China. There, specimens of the wild *Camellia japonica* can grow to an enormous size, sometimes up to 30 ft (10 m) in height – they must be a magnificent sight in the flowering season. In Europe, cultivated camellias, if left in peace, can grow into the size of small trees, with their thick shining leaves and dense growth they make excellent nesting sites for blackbirds.

The first specimens of camellias were introduced into western gardens during the early eighteenth century. They were collected from gardens in and around Canton but their early cultivation was not a success. Gardeners did not realise that camellias were hardy plants, perfectly capable of withstanding British Winters and tried to grow them in steamy hothouses where naturally they did not flourish. Most camellias are in fact exceptionally tough shrubs and will tolerate temperatures well below freezing as long as they are grown in a sheltered position.

The cushion and the picture made from the Blackbird's Nest design (see chart on page 24) are the perfect decoration for this kitchen all set ready for Easter breakfast. The yellow crown imperials and daffodils on the table are traditional Easter flowers.

1   2   3   4   5   6   7   8   9   10   11   12   13   14   15   16   17   18   19   20   21   22   23   24   25   26   27   28   29   30   31

Wool colours and quantities

The quantities listed below are the numbers of yards of Elizabeth Bradley Wool needed to work a piece measuring 165 stitches by 162 stitches on 10 mesh interlock canvas using cross stitch. There are two quantities of background wool given – one for a canvas measuring 165 stitches by 162 stitches (the size of the chart) and one for a canvas measuring 175 stitches by 172 stitches (the size of the worked examples featured in the book).

Colours used:
31 plus 1 background colour.

The background colours of the pieces shown on page 23 are pale blue (L1) and pale green (J1). The background colour used in the photograph to the right is L1.

Number on Chart key	Elizabeth Bradley Wool colour	Quantity (yards)
1	A4	17
2	A10	17
3	B2	10
4	B3	13
5	B4	14
6	B6	16
7	C2	5
8	C3	20
9	C4	16
10	C5	10
11	C7	7
12	F4	10
13	F5	11
14	F7	5
15	F8	16
16	F10	17
17	F11	15
18	G8	35
19	G9	38
20	G10	27
21	H3	12
22	H5	22
23	I3	11
24	I7	15
25	I10	15
26	J5	22
27	J6	14
28	J7	17
29	J8	19
30	K5	19
31	K6	17

Background quantity for a piece measuring 165 stitches by 162 stitches: 170 yards.

Background quantity for a piece measuring 175 stitches by 172 stitches: 200 yards.

Camellias come in many shades from deep claret to palest shell pink and glistening white. My favourites are the striped camellias developed in Second Empire France. I covet varieties such as 'Countess Lavinia Maggi' or 'Princess Clothilde' which both have white flowers boldly striped with red. I felt that such elaborate beauties might rather overwhelm The Blackbirds' Nest design and so painted the flowers in it to resemble the more restrained but equally lovely pink blooms of 'Madame Lebois', first offered for sale in 1854.

Camellias flower very early in the year and so a certain amount of poetic licence has been taken with this design. Unless Spring arrived exceptionally early it is highly unlikely that camellia flowers would be blooming coincidentally with honeysuckle and at the same time as blackbird nestlings are being fed.

Two pieces of needlework were worked as finished examples. Both were given pretty, pastel coloured, spring backgrounds, one pale blue (L1) and the other pale green (J1). An extra five rows of stitches were worked on each side and at the top and bottom of the design thus extending the size of both finished pieces to measure 17.2 inches (172 stitches) high by 17.5 inches (175 stitches) wide. These extra rows improve the look of both the finished pieces but were omitted from the chart so that the actual design part of the chart could be printed as large as possible on the page.

SPRING

The Iris

Hailstones scarred
The tender green, and
battered hard
Upon the irises, poor maids
Who fell, and died on their
own blades.

"The Death of the Irises",
Richard Church

To me, irises always mean the big bearded irises with velvet falls that flower all too briefly in late spring – the ones that we used to crush up and squeeze to make purple, iris ink when we were children. They now come in many more colours than just purple and wherever we live I make sure that I have my two favourite varieties growing in the garden: a clear apricot with bright tangerine beards called "Torch Parade" and "Lady Ilse", a pale lavender blue.

The description of irises in Gerard's *Herbal* is particularly succinct and robust, it would be difficult to better it:

"There be many kindes of Iris or Floure-de-luce, whereof some are tall and great, some little, small, and low; some smell exceeding sweet in the root, some have no smell at all. Some floures are sweet in smell, and some without: some of one colour, some of many colours mixed . . . The common Floure-de-luce hath long and large flaggy leaves like the blade of a sword with two edges, amongst which spring up smooth and plaine stalks two foot long, bearing floures toward the top compact of six leaves joyned together, wherof three that stand upright are bent inward one toward another; and in those leaves that hang downeward there are certaine rough or hairy welts, growing or rising from the nether part of the leafe upward . . . The roots be thicke, long, and knobby, with many hairy threads hanging thereat."

In Greek and Roman mythology, Iris was the goddess of the rainbow, an attribution which is particularly apt today when irises are available in almost every colour. Irises were taken as part of war booty to ancient Egypt and were painted on the walls of the palace of Knossos in Crete. Because the roots smelt so sweet they were carried in the packs of Alexander the Great's army when on campaign. This violet scented, powdered orris or iris root (*Iris florentina* or *Iris pallida*) is still used in the manufacture of perfumes and powders today.

Though Alexander's empire is long gone, the irises remain, growing wild in the countryside to mark his passing. There are many species which are native to Europe and among them is the yellow Iris or flag (*Iris pseudacorus*). This handsome but relatively undistinguished plant became the emblem of the kings of France, the Fleur de Lys, in 496. At this time, flowering yellow flags growing in shallow water in the Rhine helped King Clovis to find a fordable stretch of river and escape his enemies, the Goths. As a result, the King changed his emblem from three toads to the much more attractive – and life-saving – iris.

Specimens of the tall bearded Iris (*Iris germanica*) were collected in Asia Minor and India in the early nineteenth century. Their introduction to Western gardens led to significant advances in cultivated varieties. Most of the new varieties are a great improvement on the old, with a stronger scent and better form. Colours range from traditional yellow to orange, brown and, more recently, pink and a rusty red. A whole range of the more traditional purples is represented from Parma violet and Imperial purple to magenta and pale lavender. Some of them are a single colour while others have falls of a completely different shade. Some retain a traditionally simple shape while others are extravagantly ruffled and frilled. Somehow, however outrageous the form or colour of these new irises, they are not vulgar, the soft, blue-green, sword-like leaves and strong stems act as a restful contrast to the sometimes extravagant and bizarre flowers.

The mass of purple, blue, yellow and white irises in front of the fireplace in this picture are Spanish irises (Iris xiphium) rather than the bearded irises shown in the design on page 29. They are ideal as cut flowers and grace the flower shops every spring. On page 101 a pair of bearded irises on a pale green (J2) background can be seen as one section of a six-panel carpet.

NEEDLEWORK ANTIQUE FLOWERS

Wool colours and quantities

The quantities listed below are the number of yards of Elizabeth Bradley Wool needed to work a square measuring 160 stitches by 160 stitches on 10 mesh interlock canvas using cross stitch.

Colours used:
22 plus 1 background colour.

The background colours of the pieces shown on page 26 are blue (L5) and rich pink (A5). The background colour used in the photograph to the right is also rich pink (A5). On this piece, the word Iris has been misplaced by four stitches to the left when compared to the writing on the chart.

Number on Chart key	Elizabeth Bradley Wool colour	Quantity (yards)
1	C1	13
2	C2	17
3	C3	16
4	C4	8
5	C7	1
6	F5	19
7	F6	25
8	F8	19
9	F10	11
10	I6	11
11	I7	10
12	J3	22
13	J4	29
14	J5	33
15	K3	21
16	K5	25
17	M10	15
18	M11	10
19	N8	3
20	N9	28
21	N10	32
22	N11	29

Background quantity for a piece measuring 160 stitches by 160 stitches: 200 yards.

The Iris Design

This design shows two fine upstanding stems of the bearded iris. The flower on the right is the ancient variety "Atropurpurea" that is found in old cottage gardens and can even be seen growing wild in some parts of Britain. The bi-colour flower on the left is "Louise Watts", a comparatively recent introduction which became available in 1971. With them is a dingy brown skipper. These butterflies do not have any particular association with irises as far as I know but from a design point of view, their wings – coloured in shades of beige and brown – go very nicely with the dry, papery covering which wraps the iris buds and from which they burst into flower.

Using the chart opposite it should be possible to stitch other colours and varieties of the bearded iris instead of just the two shown below. It would be interesting to see if by changing the purples and yellows for a similar number of mauves or pinks one would end up with convincing specimens of a mauve iris like "Lace Jabot" or a pink one such as "Lovely Kay".

1   2   3   4   5   6   7   8   9   10   11   12   13   14   15   16   17   18   19   20   21   22

SPRING

Primavera

When daisies pied and
violets blue,
And lady-smocks all silver-white,
And cuckoo-buds of yellow hue
Do paint the meadows
with delight,
The cuckoo then, on every tree,
Mocks married men; for thus
sings he,
Cuckoo!
Cuckoo, cuckoo! – O word
of fear,
Unpleasing to a married ear!

"Spring and Winter", Shakespeare
(1564-1616)

Primavera is the first season of the year: in Latin it means spring. Every year we try to get away on a short holiday in late spring to see the explosion of spring flowers that occurs in parts of Italy and Greece and on many Mediterranean islands. Fields, hills and roadside verges are often completely covered by variegated carpets of wild flowers.

Primavera is a repeating design of simple spring flowers. It was inspired by a mixture of concepts and influences. First and foremost it is a celebration of flowering meadows, which are at their best in the spring before grasses and perennial plants have had a chance to grow tall. Renaissance arists also played their part in this design as they sometimes painted such meadows, scattering a world of delicate spring flowers at the feet of the Madonna and many female saints.

Further inspiration was found in the world of textiles and embroidery. First, in the stiff, formal and utterly charming representations of herbs and flowers worked by Tudor needlewomen and second, in the woven sprigs of flowers called florettes. These little portraits of simple flowers were worked into tapestries during the fifteenth and sixteenth centuries.

Renaissance Flowers

"Scatter a few Flowers and birds upon the green grass"

The Renaissance Painter, Cennini (born c. 1370)

The Renaissance heralded the return of naturalism. Artists began to look carefully at the flowers they were painting, rather than just copying what had become stylized representations of plants copied from one illustrated herbal to another. The emphasis behind flower portraits totally changed. A flower was painted to express its special and unique beauty rather than merely as a means of identifying it for medicinal or botanical purposes.

Many of the objects in Renaissance paintings are highly symbolic. For instance, a bee indicates "the golden age personified" – which is perhaps why Napoleon adopted the bee as his personal motif. A crow symbolizes hope, and a hare, lust and fecundity. Spring was often represented by a scattering of flowers on the grass, like those seen in a flowering meadow in the spring.

This symbolic concept of spring probably originated from the stories of Chloris and Zephyr. Chloris was the Greek goddess of flowers and she was married to Zephyr, the west wind of springtime. Chloris is supposed to have followed the footsteps of Zephyr in the spring, strewing the way with flowers as she went. The Romans called her Flora and Ovid tells of how Zephyr gave her a garden filled with spring flowers.

Tudor Flowers

Tudor embroidery designs were often copied from illustrations in books. In the sixteenth century, floral needlework became popular for the adornment of clothes, hangings and bed furnishings and so books of plants and herbs made a useful source of patterns. The outlines of the pictures were traced on to linen and then filled in with tiny tent or cross stitches worked in silks or fine wool.

Taste in the sixteenth century was generally quite formal; houses, clothes and furniture tended to be stiff, heavy and elaborate with even the flowers so beloved of Tudor gardeners restrained within the geometric borders of box-edged knot gardens. It is not at all surprising that the embroideries of the period followed the same trend and though beautiful and of exquisite workmanship, are equally disciplined in their design. To me they are very evocative of the interests and enthusiasms of this exceptional period when embroidery played such an important part in the

OVERLEAF: *The inspiration for Primavera was mostly historical as is reflected in this photograph. A variety of old-fashioned spring flowers are being prepared for pressing between the pages of a leather bound eighteenth-century bible found in my chapel in Wales.*

"In the middle of this garden, what seemed more delightful than anything else, was a plot of ground like a meadow; the grass of a deep green, spangled with a thousand different flowers, and set round with orange and cedar trees . . ."

The Decameron, Boccaccio (1330-75)

Tapestry Flowers

Woven tapestries were used as wall coverings in the houses of the great from the fourteenth century onwards. The finest of these hangings, or arras, were made in France. As most of the land in both France and Britain was covered with woodland and forest at that time it is not surprising that most of these tapestries showed forest glades and hunting scenes. Some, however, were flower sprigged, notably the mille-fleurs tapestries woven in France during the fifteenth and sixteenth centuries. The best known of these is the Lady with the Unicorn series of tapestries which is now in the Cluny Museum in Paris. A "thousand flowers" bloom around the feet of the three central characters, the lady, the lion and the unicorn.

This repeating Primavera design has a certain formality reminiscent of some of the flowers on these tapestries though the form of the flowers is more realistic. I felt that it was important to be able to identify each flower easily and so made the

history of some of the most famous Tudor women. Mary Queen of Scots and Bess of Hardwicke are just two of many expert needlewomen from the reign of Elizabeth I. Both were keen embroideresses much of whose work still survives to intrigue and fascinate us today.

The Primavera carpet has been finished off with a simple border worked around its edge. The chart for this border is on page 36. The central part of the carpet measures 30ins (300 stitches) by 45ins (450 stitches). The carpet complete with border measures 33.4ins (334 stitches) by 48.4ins (484 stitches).

Wool colours and quantities

The quantities listed below are the numbers of yards of Elizabeth Bradley Wool needed to work a piece measuring 150 stitches by 150 stitches on 10 mesh interlock canvas using cross stitch.

Colours used: 27 colours plus 1 background colour.

The background colour of all the Primavera pieces shown in this book is cream (F3).

Number on Chart key	Elizabeth Bradley Wool colour	Quantity (yards)
1	A2	5
2	A4	5
3	A5	4
4	A9	6
5	B2	7
6	C1	12
7	C7	4
8	D2	7
9	D4	16
10	F2	6
11	F6	9
12	F7	9
13	I2	19
14	I4	23
15	J5	19
16	J6	10
17	J9	19
18	K3	17
19	K5	26
20	L9	6
21	L10	7
22	N5	9
23	N6	5
24	N7	8
25	N8	9
26	N10	5
27	N11	5

Background quantity for a piece measuring 150 stitches by 150 stitches: 210 yards.

flowers pretty but simple, each using as few colours as possible. This restraint was both for the sake of the design, which needed to be kept uncomplicated to prevent it becoming overwhelming, and for the sake of those needleworkers who might want to work a large area with this pattern. It would have taken forever if each separate flower was too elaborate.

The Primavera Design

This design is made up of small rectangular blocks each containing a spring flower. Each block is 3ins (30 stitches) wide and 5ins (50 stitches) high.

The nine spring flowers comprise a snowdrop, a bluebell, a crocus, a cyclamen, an anemone, a daffodil, a primrose, a viola or heartsease, and a tulip.

The flowers are arranged in vertical columns with the little designs stepped so that the gap between each flower and the one above it is adjacent to the middle of a flower in the next column. The flowers are divided into three groups of three, and to make the design repeat each group should be repeated vertically up the piece of work until the required size has been reached.

Vertical columns

Group 1 snowdrop, bluebell, crocus.
Group 2 cyclamen, anemone, daffodil.
Group 3 primrose, viola, tulip.

Horizontal sequence

Across the piece the groups should progress 1, 2, 3 and then again 1, 2 and 3 and so on until the required width is achieved.

Diagonal arrangement

In order to work out which flower goes where in a new row, the diagonal arrangement of the flowers also needs to be studied. Once again, the flowers are in three groups which repeat diagonally one above the other.

Diagonal rows

Group A snowdrop, anemone, viola.
Group B bluebell, daffodil, tulip.
Group C crocus, cyclamen, primrose.
Working diagonally upwards the groups run A, B, C and then again A, B and C.

This may sound rather complicated but if studied in conjunction with the picture of the small Primavera carpet shown on page 31, it will become much clearer.

1 2 3 4 5 6 7 8 9 10 11 12 13 14 15 16 17 18 19 20 21 22 23 24 25 26 27

Wool quantities and colours

The quantities listed below are the numbers of yards of Elizabeth Bradley Wool needed to work the border of the carpet shown on page 31.

Colours used:
5 plus 1 background colour.

The background colour of the Primavera borders shown in this book is cream (F3) (except for the sampler on pages 124-5 where it has been worked against pale pink [B2]).

Elizabeth Bradley Wool colour	Quantity (yards)
A3 – pink	63
D4 – yellow	87
I4 – lime green	34
J6 – grass green	142
N7 – lilac	24

Background quantity: 150 yards.

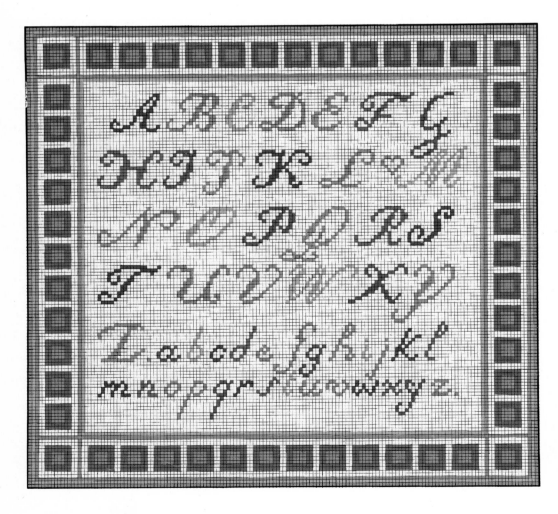

If this design is used in its stepped form as shown on this carpet and on the chart on page 35, then there are bound to be half or part flowers around the edge of the finished piece. In this way, the finished piece rather resembles a length of flowered fabric which has been cut across its pattern.

If a finished piece of needlework with no part flowers is required, it is possible to adjust the design to achieve this by moving some of the vertical groups 1, 2 or 3. Moving horizontally across a piece of needlework, move alternate groups down by half a block: 2½ ins, or 25 stitches. If, for instance, a finished piece of six blocks wide (18ins) is required, then the three vertical groups 1, 2 and 3 would need to be repeated twice, progressing across the piece from left to right

Group 1: remains stationary
Group 2: moves down by half a block
Group 3: remains stationary

Group 1: repeated, moves down half a block
Group 2: repeated, remains stationary
Group 3: repeated, moves down by half a block.

A piece worked in this way can be seen on page 34 and in the photograph on pages 32-3. It was made into a cushion which is resting on the chair towards the left of the picture.

Making the Primavera border

The border is 17 stitches wide and the last row is worked as an edging not in cross stitch (for further details see pages 98-100). The repeat is 10 rows of stitches.

This simple border has a repeat of ten stitches. It is simple to work and it is both colourful and attractive when used as an edging. It can be seen framing the Primavera carpet on page 31 and around the stitched sampler in the corner of the photograph on pages 124-5. The copperplate style alphabet in the centre was taken from an early nineteenth-century sampler and has been used for the lettering on the botanical flower designs, The Lily, The Pansy and The Cyclamen.

SPRING

Primroses in a Pot

Spring would not be spring without primroses, they are an intrinsic part of the season with their pure, sulphur yellow flowers that can be seen gleaming palely under trees and on banks and road verges all over the country. They are small, neat, perennial plants that flower in mid-spring and the yellow flowers and fresh green leaves of the native form are so pretty that many plants were taken from their natural habitat and replanted in gardens. This means that sadly, wild specimens are now not nearly as widespread as they used to be. At one time the gypsies used to collect primroses early

each year and put them in simple twig baskets lined with moss. I grew up in London, and as a child I can remember these baskets being offered for sale in the streets every spring.

Primroses symbolize youth and young love but they are also the flowers of early death. At one time their ethereal, pale yellow blooms were scattered on graves and put into coffins and perhaps for this reason, it was considered unlucky to bring the first primroses of the year into the house. Shakespeare used this association with early death in several of his plays calling the flowers "pale primroses that die unmarried" in *The Winter's Tale* and writing in *Cymbeline* – "I'll sweeten thy sad grave: thou shalt not lack the flower that's like thy face, pale primrose."

> "Cowslips and Primroses joy in moist and dankish places, but not altogether covered with water: they are found in the woods and the borders of fields. They flourish from Aprill to the end of May, and some one or other of them do floure all Winterlong."
>
> Gerard's *Herbal* (1597)

Folklore and Medicinal Properties

A varied and rather whimsical mixture of legend and folklore surrounds the flower. It was supposed to give protection against witches and so farmers hung bunches of primroses in their cowsheds to protect their animals. Eating a primrose was said to make the fairies visible and the number of petals on each flower was supposed to act as an oracle, revealing all about the state of mind of one's true love. Finding an example of the rare six petalled primrose meant good luck and was a good positive sign that generally all was well.

Like many other antique flowers, primroses were grown for their medicinal and culinary properties as well as their beauty. Their juice, when rubbed on the face, helped to remove spots and blemishes. Syrup of primrose roots was used as a remedy for headaches and palsy, and when sniffed up the nose it caused beneficial sneezing. Like violets they can

Ask me why I send you here
This sweet Infanta of the year?
Ask me why I send to you
This primrose, thus bepearl'd
with dew?
I will whisper to your ears:-
The sweets of love are mix'd
with tears.

"The Primrose", Robert Herrick
(1591-1674)

be crystallized in sugar and used as sweets and cake decorations.

The name primrose is derived from the diminutive of primavera, primaverola, meaning the first flower of spring. This later became primarole and by Elizabethan times, primarose. Primroses are truly antique flowers and some varieties have been cultivated in gardens for hundreds of years. Double primroses and varieties such as Hose-in-Hose and Jack-in-the-Greens were great favourites in Tudor gardens. They were particularly valuable in the small box-edged beds of knot gardens because they flowered so early.

Primroses are supposed to be easy to grow but I find them difficult to keep from year to year. I suspect that they thrive on poor conditions, natural humus and healthy neglect rather than little meals of bonemeal and anxious glances whenever they look a bit limp. Apparently, this sort of over-indulgence is not uncommon among gardeners and at one time so many plants of the rarer varieties were being killed by the kindness of enthusiasts that stocks became quite depleted.

The native pale yellow primrose is sometimes seen on old embroideries, especially those from the Tudor period, but it is the more showy and elaborate flowers of the polyanthus and the auricula that appear in almost every bunch of flowers stitched in the eighteenth and nineteenth centuries. The strong colours and distinct shape of their blooms make them much easier to portray than the simple delicate blooms of the primrose.

"In dewy glades, The peering primrose, like
a sudden gladness gleams on the soul."

Samuel Taylor Coleridge (1772-1834)

The Primrose Design

The simple native primrose remains my favourite in the primula family despite strong competition from auriculas and laced polyanthus. This Primrose in a Pot design shows a flourishing primrose plant growing in a terracotta pot. The pot rests on a dark, olive-green base and is set against a background of soft pink, gingham checks. The completed needlework could be framed as a picture for a country bedroom or kitchen, or if the background and base are extended sideways to make the piece into a squarer shape it would make a very pretty cushion. A whole row of Primroses in Pots would make an amusing seat cover for a settle or long stool.

Two such pots were combined to make a long, pillow-shaped cushion which is shown on the bed in the photograph opposite. For a change, they were worked against a background stitched in two shades of grey rather than pink. Although the pots and the leaves of each plant are identical the flowers are not, one has pink flowers and the other the usual pale yellow.

If primroses are required in colours other than yellow then all that is needed are three close shades of the relevant colours for the petals. The centres, worked in two shades of yellow with pale green in the middle, remain the same. Simple single primroses come in many colours and so there is plenty of scope with nearly 100 named varieties to chose from and more being developed all the time. To give just a few, "Afterglow" is rusty orange, "Anita" navy blue, "Appleblossom" a pale pink, and "Belle de Jardines" a rosy red. Other colours include mauve, crimson, claret, magenta, lilac, white and even green.

Pale yellow and soft peachy pink primroses in "long Tom" terracotta flowerpots are shown in a child's country bedroom.

1   2   3   4   5   6   7   8   9   10   11   12   13   14   15   16   17   18   19   20   21

Wool colours and quantities

The quantities given below are the numbers of yards of Elizabeth Bradley Wool needed to work a piece measuring 130 stitches by 156 stitches on 10 mesh interlock canvas using cross stitch.

Colours used: 21 colours including 2 background colours.

The background colours used in the framed piece on page 37 are peachy pinks (B2 and B4). The background colours used in the framed picture on page 39 are peachy pinks (B2 and B4) and on the pillow on the bed they are soft greys (H1 and H2)

Number on Chart key	Elizabeth Bradley Wool colour	Quantity (yards)
1	A9	24
2	A10	19
3	B2	59
4	B4	50
5	D2	11
6	C2	22
7	D4	10
8	D6	7
9	D9	8
10	G5	8
11	G8	3
12	I1	12
13	I4	25
14	I7	16
15	I8	34
16	I10	25
17	J3	7
18	J4	7
19	J6	22
20	J7	15
21	J8	5

The colour of the background can also be changed. To give a soft subtle effect, work the background in two close shades of whatever colour is required. A bolder background can be achieved by using white or cream wool (F2 or F3) with another colour such as French blue (L11) or a soft lavender blue (M6) both of which would be pretty and fresh.

Key numbers 3, 4, 5, 6 and 7 can be changed depending on the colour of primroses and background that are required. Numbers 3 and 4 on the key are the background colours (either B2 and B4 or H1 and H2). Numbers 5, 6 and 7 are the colours of the primrose flowers, D2, C2 and D4 being used in the yellow primroses and B2, A1 and A3 in the pink primroses.

When working the double piece (two Pots of Primroses) 5 stitches were omitted from the adjoining sides of both charts so that in the centre the gingham pattern is unaltered but the pots are slightly closer together. When more than one Pot of Primroses is worked on a single piece of woolwork the design looks more balanced with this reduced gap between the pots.

SPRING

A Bunch of Spring Flowers

In the last month of May
I made her posies;
I heard her often say
That she loved roses.
Cowslips and gillyflowers
and the white lily
I brought to deck the bowers
For my sweet Philly.

"Phillada flouts Me", Anon

Most of the spring flowers in this brightly coloured bunch or bouquet tied with blue ribbons have been grown in cottage gardens for hundreds of years. They are all bulbs or perennial plants, demanding little attention and coming up at the beginning of each year to delight us with their freshness and colour after the winter. Small bunches of flowers used to be called posies or tussie mussies, sometimes the name nosegay was used for the obvious reason that the scent of the flowers helped to disguise the unpleasant smells that were part of daily living. The lilac, violets, sweet rocket and narcissus which are included in this nosegay are all strongly and sweetly scented.

Flowers for Weddings and Gifts

Many customs and traditions involve the carrying of bunches of flowers. Brides invariably carried simple sheaves of seasonal blooms like this one at their weddings until much more elaborate lace-trimmed posies and wired bouquets of orange blossom and jasmine were introduced in Victorian times. Seventeenth-century French bridegrooms took their floral duties very seriously and sent their brides a nosegay of the finest flowers every day until the marriage took place. Traditionally, the Queen is given a nosegay of fragrant herbs and spring flowers on Maundy Thursday each year, and at one time judges used to carry scented posies of flowers into court. A more surprising custom was the large bunches of flowers given to condemned men to carry on their last walk or ride to the gallows. "Methinks I see him already in the Cart, sweeter and more lovely than the Nosegay in his Hand", sings Polly Peachum about her highwayman lover, Macheath, in *The Beggar's Opera* which first opened in 1728.

Today, bunches of flowers are used as unexceptional gifts for all sorts of occasions; they convey appreciation, thanks, sympathy or admiration. As presents they are on a par with a box of chocolates, being not too personal, but having the advantage of being a lot less fattening.

What is in a Bunch?

For those who are style conscious there can be subtle distinctions between one bunch of flowers and another, these constantly change as flowers go in and out of fashion. At the moment, auriculas are so popular that they are almost in danger of over exposure. Other flowers such as gold-laced polyanthus, pale creamy daffodils and striped Darwin or extravagantly frilled parrot tulips are considered smart, whereas bright pink or mauve lily-flowered tulips are definitely out of favour. White, green or pale pastel flowers are a safe choice, they are always delicate and pretty.

> "A lady would as soon think of having a pig in a parlour, as a ramping spike of Hollyhock in a bouquet; and even a coachman, who on state days is expected to wear a nosegay as large as a cauliflower, would look awkward with six feet of Hollyhock stuck in his button hole."

The Gardener and Practical Florist (1843)

In 1824, flowers were out of fashion altogether. Henry Phillips, the flower historian wrote, "Fashion does not at present sanction any but coachmen in wearing nosegays in this country, yet it has not influence sufficient to banish flowers from the garden." Thankfully, for the survival of many species of garden plants, flowers soon came back into favour.

This French armoire is a treasure house of pattern and colour. Lengths and samples of fabrics and ribbons pack the shelves. Two pieces of needlework made from the A Bunch of Spring Flowers chart on page 45 can be seen on the shelves.

Wool colours and quantities

The quantities listed below are the numbers of yards of Elizabeth Bradley Wool needed to work a piece measuring 204 stitches by 211 stitches on 10 mesh interlock canvas using cross stitch.

Colours used:
32 including 2 background colours (Key numbers 20 and 32, below).

Number on Chart key	Elizabeth Bradley Wool colour	Quantity (yards)
1	A1	8
2	A6	38
3	A7	30
4	B11	17
5	C1	17
6	C3	19
7	C5	11
8	C7	8
9	D4	20
10	F5	22
11	H4	3
12	H5	5
13	I1	13
14	I2	15
15	I4	28
16	I8	12
17	J5	21
18	J6	22
19	J8	16
20	L8	16
21	L9	47
22	L10	30
23	L11	14
24	M10	17
25	M11	14
26	N5	14
27	N6	15
28	N7	10
29	N9	5
30	N10	9
31	N11	14
32	F3	17

Background quantity of Key number 32, cream (F3), for a piece measuring 204 stitches by 211 stitches: 330 yards.

The Language of Flowers

The giving of a bunch of flowers in the mid- and late nineteenth century could be something of a nightmare. The language of flowers had become a cult, each flower had its own meaning and not only the recipient, but everybody else as well knew what that meaning was. Great care had to be taken not to compromise a girl or to unwittingly propose with a bunch of flowers. Jilting or breaking an engagement was regarded very seriously and could be cause for litigation. Bunches of pasque flowers with their message "You have no claim", must have come in useful at such times.

The meaning of the individual flowers in this particular bunch of spring blooms was certainly not taken into consideration when it was painted. However, as an interesting exercise I looked them all up in my small Victorian copy of *The Language of Flowers* and here they are: anemone means forsaken, daffodil means regard, purple lilac means unrequited love. A narcissus means egotism, a yellow primrose sadness and early death, and a red primrose, unappreciated merit. A striped tulip means beautiful eyes. Dame's violet or sweet rocket means watchfulness, violets mean modesty. Wallflowers mean fidelity in adversity, blue vinca or periwinkle means early friendship and forget-me-not, of course, means forget-me-not. After analysis of all these meanings, this bunch of flowers would seem to be suitable for a not very confident but hopeful swain to give to a girl with beautiful eyes. On reflection, he might have been wiser to leave the primrose out altogether!

Embroidered Bouquets

Shakespeare used flowers allegorically in many of his plays, their meanings were well known in Tudor times and no doubt Tudor needlewomen bore them in mind when deciding on the flowers to include in an embroidered bouquet. Many delightful nosegays worked with floss silks on cream silk backgrounds were worked in the late eighteenth century. The stems of the flowers are almost invariably held together with a length of pale blue ribbon tied in a bow. Berlin woolwork bunches of flowers were equally popular with Victorian embroideresses who stitched their roses, lilies and forget-me-nots with brightly coloured wool on canvas. Sometimes, the background area was left bare but more often it was filled in with stitches. Black or cream were the commonest background colours. This bunch of woolwork flowers has been given a cream background enlivened with pale blue spots.

This design is rather large for a cushion but it is perfect for putting into a fire-screen or for using on a stool. The size can be adjusted by working more or less of the blue spotted background until the required area is covered.

Note: Key number 20, pale blue (L8), is used for the blue spots in the background. The quantity given in the table to the left shows the wool used for these spots. Key number 32, cream (F3), is used as the main background colour as well as in the design. The quantity given in the table to the left is for the amount of wool used in the design only. The background quantity of Key number 32, cream (F3), is given separately, below the table.

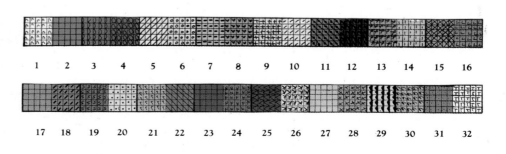

| 1 | 2 | 3 | 4 | 5 | 6 | 7 | 8 | 9 | 10 | 11 | 12 | 13 | 14 | 15 | 16 |

| 17 | 18 | 19 | 20 | 21 | 22 | 23 | 24 | 25 | 26 | 27 | 28 | 29 | 30 | 31 | 32 |

Working with Borders

There are charts for five borders inlcuded in this book, two are wide and elaborate and three are narrow and simple. The wide borders are The Sunflower Border on pages 70-1 and The Nasturtium and Butterfly Border on page 97, both have instructions and diagrams with them to assist in their use. The three narrow borders are below and on pages 36 and 117.

As a general rule, it is much easier to adapt the size of a piece of needlework that forms the central area inside a border than it is to change the border itself. The zig-zag border on this page has a repeat of eight stitches while the other two have repeats of ten stitches. All that this means is that the centrepieces of these borders should measure a multiple of either eight or ten stitches. The centrepiece may fit its intended border exactly, but if it does not, it will need to be adapted by adding or subtracting a few rows of background or pattern until it is the correct size.

These narrow borders make useful and decorative edgings for small carpets or for adding extra embellishment to a cushion. Alernatively, they can be used as strips of needlework for making belts and braces, or straps for bags and cameras.

This simple zigzag border, worked in four shades of blue on a cream (F3) background, has a repeat of eight stitches. It can be seen used as the handle to a bag on pages 12-13, and as a pair of braces, a case for a couple of pencils and a border for a stitched sampler on pages 124-5. The classic alphabet in the centre can be seen on many late eighteenth- and early nineteenth-century samplers, and it is one of my favourites.

SUMMER

SUMMER

Come into the garden, Maud,
For the black bat, Night,
has flown,
Come into the garden, Maud,
I am here at the gate alone;
And the woodbine spices are
wafted abroad,
And the musk of the roses
blown . . .

There has fallen a splendid tear
From the passion-flower at the
gate,
She is coming, my dove, my dear;
She is coming, my life, my fate;
The red rose cries, "She is near,
she is near;"
And the white rose weeps,
"She is late;"
The larkspur listens, "I hear,
I hear;"
And the lily whispers, "I wait".

"Maud", Alfred, Lord Tennyson
(1809-92)

Summer brings the reward for a whole year's hard work. By the beginning of the season, the garden is up and growing, the roses are sprayed, the flower-beds fed and filling up, the delphiniums staked and everything ready for the main explosion of flowers that culminates in mid-summer. The roses, from being merely promising buds explode into full flower, mats of pinks and border carnations and tangles of cream and apricot honeysuckle exude great waves of scent into the evening air.

The euphoria of high summer is a very personal satisfaction for a gardener, but it is also a good time of year to go and visit other people's gardens. It is interesting to study different garden designs and planting schemes, whether antique or modern, and to note particularly good varieties of roses and other favourite plants.

Antique Summer Flowers

Many gardeners are interested in the history of their plants as well as their appearance and this is the season of many of the truly antique flowers, some of which are called florists' flowers. These pampered florists' species were transformed or per-fected to the most extreme degree and often bear little relation to the simple native plants from which they were bred. Pinks, carnations and violas are true florists' flowers while lilies, delphiniums, peonies, poppies, roses and sweet peas are examples of antique summer flowers which have also been the subject of extensive changes and im-provements over a long period of time. Most of these flowers have their own societies and series of shows which culminate in an annual show when each species is at its flowering peak. Each society has its own rules, aims and standards of excellence

and competition can be fierce in the attempt to attain perfection.

Antique and florists' flowers often have fasci-nating histories and stories associated with them. Some have very aristocratic connections while others have always been cottagers' or working men's favourites. Sadly, it is impossible to cover the history of more than a few of them in such a book as this. The story of the pansy is described on page 108, the poppy on page 64, and the lily on pages 56-9. Other flowers are mentioned in their seasons, for example, the hellebore and cyclamen are discussed in "Winter", and the primrose and iris in "Spring".

Many of these antique flowers have been with us for so long that they have become great favourites. They are part of our heritage and folk memory and are found in the majority of gardens even if the in-dividual gardener has no idea of their history or im-portance as medicinal plants. On the whole, it was their seeds and roots that were carried by colonists, along with the more essential herb, cereal and vegetable seeds to many parts of the globe. Favourite flowering plants thus travelled to the New World with their owners and with them went the scent and memories of the summer gardens of home.

All sorts of roots and herbes in gardens grow,
Parsnips, carrots, turnips, or what you'll sow,
Onions, melons, cucumbers, radishes,
Skirrets, beets, coleworts, and fair cabbages.
Here grow fine flowers many and 'mongst those,
The fair white lily and sweet fragrant rose.

Governor William Bradford of Plymouth Plantation
from the *Descriptive and Historical account of New England
in Verse.*

PREVIOUS PAGE: *A hot day, a long drink and lots of ice, comfortable cushions to recline on and
sunflower and pumpkin seeds to eat – an ideal way to spend a summer's afternoon. The square
cushions and the long flowered strips are made from The Sunflower Border design from pages 70-71.
The centre of the large cushion and the whole of the smaller one were made using the Provençal Centre
chart on page 70. The square placemat and the round cushion were made from the Sunflower Circle
design on page 63.*

Embroidered Summer Flowers

The classic flowers of summer are the ones most often found on historical embroidery both in Britain and America. Borders of roses, honeysuckle and pinks edge samplers in the New World just as they do here. Records and descriptions of many pieces of sixteenth-, seventeenth- and eighteenth-century embroidery exist in both countries even if the actual pieces of needlework have long since disappeared.

Tudor embroiderers obviously loved flowers whatever the season. On one panel at Traquair House in Scotland there are 61 different flowers arranged in ordered rows. They include classic summer flowers such as roses, cornflowers, lilies, marigolds and pinks as well as spring flowers and various fruit and vegetables. Mary Queen of Scots must have missed flowers dreadfully during her long years in captivity and sewed many varieties into her numerous pieces of needlework. In 1574, she sent a skirt of crimson satin as a gift to Queen Elizabeth. It was decorated with finely worked flowers of honeysuckle, pinks, and lilies, and it also featured roses for England, thistles for Scotland and daffodils for Wales.

Only a description remains of a petticoat that belonged to Mrs Delany early in the eighteenth century. This fascinating lady was an enthusiastic diarist as well as a keen gardener and an expert at all sorts of crafts. She left numerous descriptions of the clothes and happenings of her day as well as nearly one thousand portraits of different flowers made from cut paper which she made between the ages of 73 and 82 years. These are now in the British Museum.

One petticoat belonging to Mrs Delany was described by Lady Llanover as being:

"covered with sprays of natural flowers, in different positions, including the burgloss, auriculas, honeysuckle, wild roses, lilies of the valley, yellow and white jessamine, interspersed with small single flowers. The border at the bottom being entirely composed of large flowers in the manner in which they grow, both garden and wild flowers being intermingled where the form, proportions and foliage rendered it desirable for the effect of the whole."

Another petticoat belonging to the Duchess of Queensbury sounds even more bizarre:

". . . the bottom of the petticoat brown hills covered with all sorts of weeds, and every breadth had an old stump of a tree that run up almost to the top of the petticoat, broken and ragged and worked with brown chenille, round which twined nastersians, evy, honeysuckles, periwinkles, convolvuluses and all sorts of twining flowers which spread and covered the petticoat, vines with the leaves variegated as you have seen them by the sun, all rather smaller than nature . . . the robings and facings were little green banks with all sorts of weeds, and the sleeves and the rest of the gown loose twining branches of the same sort as those on the petticoat: many of the leaves were finished with gold, and part of the stumps of the trees looked like the golding of the sun. I never saw a work so prettily fancied, and am quite angry with myself for not having the same thought, for it is infinitely handsomer than mine, and could not cost much more."

Mrs Delany – Her Life and Her Flowers,
Ruth Hayden.

Such extraordinary, embroidered extravaganzas epitomize for me the close and sometimes eccentric link between the lovers of gardening and flowers and embroidery. Only a fanatical gardener would think of stitching a whole summer garden complete with weeds and a decorative tree stump on to a dress. Mrs Delany would have been a fascinating person to talk to. I would like to have met her.

The Summer Sampler

Silk colours and quantities

The quantities listed below are the number of skeins of DMC six-stranded perle cotton needed to work a sampler 163 stitches by 163 stitches. Each length of cotton should be split in half and the sampler worked with three strands only.

The sampler shown opposite was worked on 100% linen scrim, 91cms wide which has approximately 20 threads to the inch. Each stitch should be worked over two threads.

Number on Chart key	DMC thread number	Number of skeins
1	761	1
2	760	2
3	3712	1
4	780	1
5	834	3
6	833	1
7	ecru	3
8	644	4
9	612	2-3
10	3021	3
11	648	3
12	647	3
13	988	2
14	367	2
15	580	4
16	3362	3
17	928	2
18	926	1-2
19	3750	1
20	3042	1-2
21	3041	1

A virgin that's industrious, Merits Praise,
N ature she Imitates in Various Ways,
N ow forms the Pink, now gives the Rose its blaze.

Y oung Buds, she folds, in tender Leaves of green,
O mits no shade to beautify her Scene.
U pon the Canvas, see, the Letters rise,
N eatly they shine with intermingled dies,
G lide into Words, and strike us with Surprize.

A verse from a sampler dated 1749

Many of the most charming antique samplers have pictures of houses and gardens embroidered upon them. Parks rather than flower gardens were usual on eighteenth- and early nineteenth-century samplers for this was the time when landscape gardening was all the rage. Most sampler houses are built of red brick or stone, they tend to be Queen Anne or Georgian in style, and they generally stand on a green hill or are set in a park elaborated with fencing, deer and trees. Occasionally, the house on a sampler is obviously modelled on a real house but more often it was copied from a pattern.

. . . The timid maid
Pleasd to be praisd and yet of praise affraid
Seeks her best flowers not those of woods
and fields
But such as every farmers garden yield
Fine cabbage roses painted like her face
And shining pansys trimmd in golden lace
And tall tuft larksheels featherd thick wi flowers
And woodbines climbing oer the door in bowers
The London tufts of many a mottld hue
And pale pink pea and monkshood darkly blue
And white and purple jiliflowers that stay
Lingering in blossom summer half away
And single blood walls of a luscious smell
Old fashioned flowers which huswives
love so well
And columbines stone blue or deep night brown
Their honey-comb-like blossoms hanging down
Each cottage gardens fond adopted child . . .

The Shepherd's Calendar for June, John Clare (1827)

The house on this summer sampler is one of many standard sampler houses. In a scale of grandness, it would probably be classed as a large cottage in comparison with some of the mansions that appear. This particular house is invariably shown complete with wall and gateposts and a path of some kind. It often appears on Scottish samplers and all the examples on which I have seen it worked are of excellent quality. They were all sewn between 1750 and 1800 and so the pattern must have appeared in this period.

The Summer Sampler

Since this is a twentieth-century sampler it has a flower garden. Garden styles have changed and herbaceous borders grown in the manner of mixed Victorian and cottage garden flowerbeds are once more fashionable. The house is set in such a garden and the beds are crowded with brightly coloured summer flowers. The sun is shining and a cloud of honey bees have emerged from an old fashioned, straw beehive on one side of the garden. A checkered path leads from the front door to the gateway. Daisies flower in the grass verges outside the garden wall, a small black dog of mixed parentage stands on the path enjoying the sun.

The sort of garden shown on this sampler was a very popular subject for embroidery in the 1930s and 1940s. Idealized cottage gardens were stitched onto hundreds of tea cosies, cushions and pictures. The cottage itself was usually thatched and complete with beams, geraniums on the windowsill and flowered curtains. The flowers themselves were often worked in a mixture of stitches including French knots, lazy daisy, chain stitch and many others.

In a very romantic description of such cottage gardens, WH Hudson in *From a Shepherd's Life* describes how cottages "stand among, and are wrapped in, flowers as a garment – rose and vine and creeper and clematis. They are mostly thatched, but some have tiled roofs, their deep,

A frame of bright and pretty mid-summer flowers surrounds this sampler. They were selected from the vast choice of summer flowering plants that burgeon and bloom at this time of year.

Wool colours and quantities

The quantities listed below are the numbers of yards of Elizabeth Bradley Wool needed to work a piece measuring 169 stitches by 169 stitches on 10 mesh interlock canvas using cross stitch.

Colours used:
21 plus 1 background colour.

When working the woolwork on the right from the chart opposite, the pink line border was omitted and four extra rows of background colour were worked around the edges.

The background colour used in the piece shown on page 2 is black (G11).

Number on Chart key	Elizabeth Bradley Wool colour	Quantity (yards)
1	A2	12
2	A3	20
3	A4	12
4	C6	4
5	D4	17
6	D6	6
7	F3	6
8	F5	54
9	F6	42
10	G9	10
11	H7	12
12	H8	24
13	J4	29
14	J5	34
15	J6	45
16	J8	15
17	L8	25
18	L9	20
19	L10	9
20	N9	20
21	N10	9

Background quantity for a piece measuring 169 stitches by 169 stitches: 150 yards.

dark red clouded and stained with lichen and moss; and these roofs, too, have their flowers in summer. They are grown over with yellow stonecrop, that bright cheerful flower that smiles down at you from the lowly roof above the door . . . But its garden flowers, clustering and nestling round it, amid which its feet are set – they are to me the best of all flowers. These are the flowers we know and re-member forever. The old, homely, cottage-garden blooms, so old that they have entered the soul . . . fragrant gillyflower and pink and clove-smelling carnation; wallflower, abundant periwinkle, sweet-william, larkspur, love-in-a-mist, and love-lies-bleeding . . . and kiss-me-John-at-the-garden-gate, sometimes called pansy."

Samplers from the eighteenth century often have delicate borders of naturalistic flowers worked in long and short stitch. Cross stitch floral borders tended to be more formal and repetitive. This cross stitch border is somewhere between the two. It shows a mixture of roses, blue convolvulus, forget-me-nots and mauve coloured pinks.

1 2 3 4 5 6 7 8 9 10 11 12 13 14 15 16 17 18 19 20 21

SUMMER

The Lily

Where did Gabriel get a lily
In the month of March,
When the green
Is hardly seen
On the early larch?
Though I know
Just where they grow,
I have pulled no daffodilly.

Where did Gabriel get a lily
In the month of March.
Could I bring
The tardy spring
Under her foots arch,
Near and far
The primrose star
Should bloom with violets,
willy nilly.
Where did Gabriel get a lily
In the month of March.

"Lady Day", G James

Lilies are magnificent flowers, tall, stately and impressive. Fragrant and shapely flowers with waxy petals and long golden anthers, thick with pollen, are held on stiff stems embellished along their length with glossy, dark green, lanceolate leaves. The flowers are arranged in loose and graceful bunches crowning stems that can grow to a majestic 10ft (3m) in some species.

These plants are interesting and exciting flowers at all stages of their growth; the bulbs are fat and fleshy, the shoots impressively large and the growth very rapid. The buds are long and graceful, the flowers splendid and even the seed heads add interest to a border.

Lilies have been brought to Western gardens from many exotic parts of the world. Many beautiful species were collected in the wild and brought back to Europe by intrepid and determined plant collectors. The delightful and easily grown *Lilium regale* was found growing in great scented drifts in a remote valley in northwest China by Ernest H Wilson. He nearly died trying to bring bulbs back to Britain and regarded the introduction of this lily as the supreme achievement of his life.

"Royal is this lily and regally it has taken its
place and added lustre to gardens. Proud
am I to have discovered, introduced and
christened the Regal Lily. – Did what?

God forgive me! No I didn't.
Tis God's present to our gardens.
Anybody might have found it but –
His whisper came to me!"
(with apologies to Kipling)

Plant Hunting, Ernest H Wilson (1927)

Some lilies originate nearer to home and our native, European species have their own particular charm. They include the glistening, pure white,

Madonna lily which seems to thrive best in cottage gardens. The Martagon and Turkscap lilies are exotics with curly turned back petals, and the orange spotted Tiger Lily who talked to Alice in the book *Alice in Wonderland* by Lewis Carroll is another home bred charmer.

The "Stargazer" Lily

Recently, even more splendid and very well behaved varieties of lily have come to us through the processes of breeding and hybridization. The lily "Stargazer" is one of the prettiest of these new hybrids and was used as the model for the lily design in this book. It was developed and bred in California and launched on to the market in 1975. "Stargazer" has been an outstandingly successful new introduction due to its elegant and graceful form of growth. The flowers are held on long stems and each faces upwards towards the sun; every stem – whether picked for the house or left growing in the garden – seems to arrange itself to perfection. The petals are coloured pink or cherry red with a white, frilly edge and burgundy spots. The pistil of each flower is long and green and the anthers are a rich golden orange. The leaves are wider than in other varieties and are of a dark and glossy green. The buds are a glistening shell pink with pale lemon tips when they are young. "Stargazer" will flower from quite small bulbs and is happy either growing in a pot or out in the garden.

History of the Lily

The lily is one of the oldest flowers in existence with some species dating from before the last ice age. Due to the great beauty of its flowers and usefulness as a medicinal plant it has been cultivated by man from the very beginnings of civilization. The lily has been acclaimed in both literature and art and a rich collection of myth, lore and legend

"Stargazer" lilies, both real and stitched. This splendid lily always looks attractive in any sort of flower arrangement. The woolwork lily can be worked from the chart on page 58. The background colour used for the piece shown here is red (A6) and on page 59 it is black (G11).

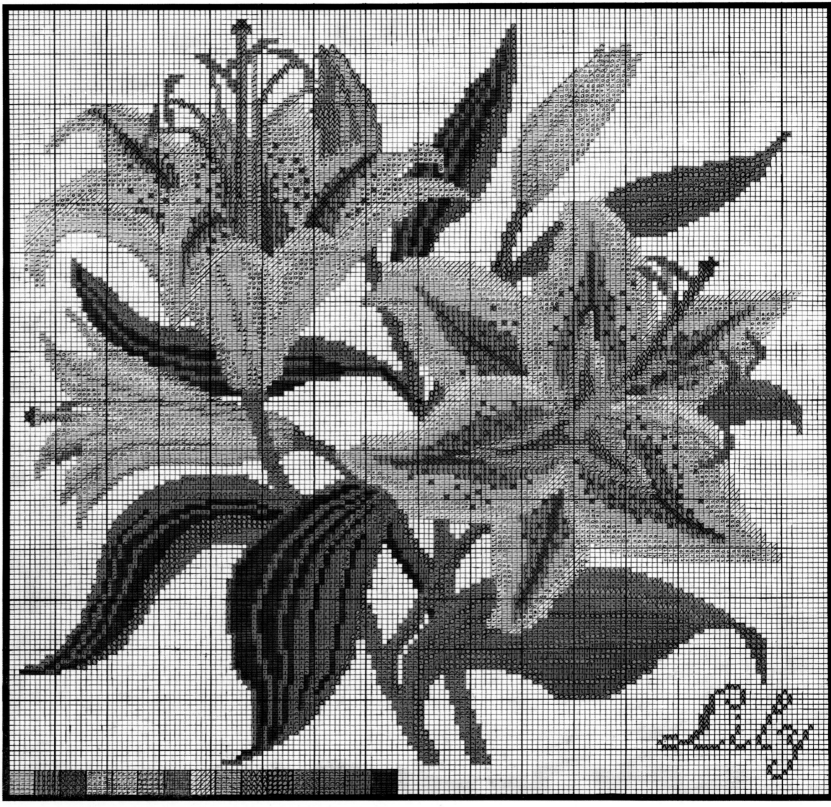

1   2   3   4   5   6   7   8   9   10   11   12   13   14   15

of innocence, purity and majesty and the flower most associated with the Virgin Mary, this lily takes precedence over all other flowers in Christian art. It appears again and again in paintings, either on its own, or placed in the hands of female saints and angels. In portrayals of the Annunciation, the Archangel Gabriel is often shown holding a lily to symbolize the purity of the Madonna. The charming poem on page 56 questions how a lily was found in March.

Embroidered Lilies

With such a distinguished history, it is not surprising that the lily also features prominently on many pieces of needlework. Traditionally, rich fabrics and embroidery have always been used to adorn churches. Vestments, altar frontals and banners were often embellished with embroidered lilies and they are still stitched on to pieces of ecclesiastical needlework today. Lilies were sewn on to dresses, doublets and hangings throughout the Tudor period and can often be found on samplers and embroidered pictures. They appear in the embroidered versions of the Dutch flower paintings of the early eighteenth century and in the pretty beribboned baskets of mixed flowers so beloved of French needlewomen later in the century.

The Victorians were really enthusiastic about their lilies and all sorts of exotic spotted varieties appear on Berlin woolwork charts. Cross stitch studies of the pure white Madonna and Arum lilies were also popular, the connection of the flower with innocence and purity no doubt appealing to the more sentimental side of the Victorian nature. They also appear in embroideries of the Arts and Crafts period and it is only comparatively recently that they seem to have gone rather out of favour. No doubt their time will come again and they will once more be as popular on pieces of woolwork and embroidery as they are in our gardens.

> "The Rose sleeps in her beauty, but the lily seems unaware of her own exceeding loveliness"
>
> *The Scented Garden*, Eleanor Sinclair Rohde

Wool colours and quantities

The quantities listed below are the numbers of yards of Elizabeth Bradley Wool needed to work a piece measuring 160 stitches by 160 stitches on 10 mesh interlock canvas using cross stitch.

Colours used: 15 colours plus 1 background colour.

Number on Chart key	Elizabeth Bradley Wool colour	Quantity (yards)
1	A2	35
2	A4	20
3	A6	12
4	B2	35
5	C1	24
6	C3	11
7	C7	8
8	D2	15
9	I3	15
10	I6	15
11	I9	24
12	J6	15
13	J7	24
14	J8	24
15	K6	24

Background quantity for a piece measuring 160 stitches by 160 stitches: 240 yards.

has grown up around it over the centuries. Most of this body of knowledge is associated with the ancient white lily, *Lilium candidum*, or Madonna lily. The Egyptians regarded this plant as sacred while the Greeks dedicated it to Hera, the Goddess of light and the sky. In Roman legend, Madonna lilies were supposed to have grown from a few drops of milk that fell to earth from Juno's breast while she suckled the infant Hercules. The Christians – not to be outdone – believed that it sprang up from the repentant tears of Eve as she fled from the Garden of Eden.

A lily appears in the golden crown of the Byzantine Empress Theodora in 537 and the Venerable Bede, who died in 737, made it the symbol of the Resurrection of the Virgin Mary – when she ascended to heaven she left behind her a tomb filled with Madonna lilies and roses. As the symbol

---

NOTE: *Please work the designs for The Lily (left), The Pansy (page 113) and The Cyclamen (page 150) to the outer edge of the thick black line.*

SUMMER

Circles of Bright Summer Flowers

Just now the lilac is in bloom,
All before my little room;
And in my flower-beds, I think,
Smile the carnation and the pink;
And down the borders,
well I know,
The poppy and the pansy
blow . . .

"Grantchester", Rupert Brooke
(1887-1915)

Summer flowers can be grouped into colours as well as varieties. Single colour flowerbeds and borders with delicate pale colours were made fashionable by gardeners such as Vita Sackville-West in her garden at Sissinghurst in Kent and by the famous late Victorian gardener Gertrude Jekyll. Arrangements of white and pastel shades, purples, pale blues and pinks, grey foliage and variegated leaves have been popular ever since – such colours are indeed very restful in a baking hot, summer garden.

Having made my own attempt at a mini Sissinghurst in our last garden, which was large, I have now reverted to a vulgar mix of colour in my flowerbeds. I suspect that small gardens make one less fussy and they can be boring if too refined. A whole summer of pale pink and white, with no other bit of garden to wander in, would be very tedious. Unadulterated bright orange flowers, except for marigolds and nasturtiums, are still banned but I have become quite fond of other brilliantly coloured blooms in small doses.

The recent spate of hot summers encourages the growing of bright coloured flowers like those found on flower stalls in French markets. I spent much time on a recent holiday to France gazing with delight at buckets bursting with brilliant and clashing colours. Sunflowers, marigolds, zinnias, cornflowers, snapdragons, larkspur, sweet peas and many other brightly coloured annuals were all massed together in stunning displays.

Having despised such annual flowers for years as being a waste of time compared to perennials, I am now converted. There are so many attractive varieties to choose from and different ones can be grown from seed each year. Planted between the permanent shrubs and herbaceous plants they provide colour, interest and scent in July and August when the first flush of summer flowers are finished. Growing annuals is both interesting and a good way of achieving freshness and change in a small garden.

Some years, a selection of rarities can be attempted if one is organized and orders seed early. My favourite annuals at the moment are more pedestrian, however, and their seed can be purchased from any mixed rack. This year, for the first time, I have planted love-lies-bleeding; with its weird crimson or lime green flowers like cat's tails, it should add interest to tired, late summer beds. The green zinnia, "Envy", is an on-going favourite, but unfortunately the snails love it as much as I do, so that I am now left with one solitary pot-full. I plant nicotiana every year for the scent of the flowers in the early evening, while nasturtiums come up in unexpected places in the garden whether I sow them or not.

Pansies are perennial plants but are best treated as annuals and grown from seed every year. If sown early in the spring they will flower the same year. Pansy seed germinates well and they are easy plants to grow but they flower so energetically all summer that they exhaust themselves and so are difficult to keep going from year to year. This year, I planted seeds of "Joker Light Blue" with pale, lavender blue petals and a white and purple face. I also sowed several packets of mixed hybrid pansies from which flowers in interesting shades of tawny, rust, crimson and purple might grow.

Sweet peas are another scented annual and summer would not be the same without them. There are so many lovely varieties to choose from, both old and new, that they need never become dull and repetitive. I need my garden walls for clematis, roses and honeysuckle and so this year the sweet peas are planted in two very smart green wirework pyramids each about 6ft (2m) tall – I am hoping these will soon become totally covered with scented and brightly-coloured flowers.

Lots of small bags, purses, pincushions, sleep and travel pillows made from the Flower Circle designs on pages 63, 65 and 67.

SUMMER

Sunflower Circle

Wool colours and quantities

The quantities listed below are the numbers of yards of Elizabeth Bradley Wool needed to work a square piece with a border as seen on the chart opposite. It measures 132 stitches by 132 stitches and has been worked on 10 mesh interlock canvas using cross stitch.

Colours used: 13 colours including 1 background colour. Key number 13 is the background colour, dark green (J9).

As mentioned in the text, the chart can be used to make a circular or a square piece. The circular piece only uses 11 colours plus the background colour because Key number 9, brown (E9), occurs in the border only.

Number on Chart key	Elizabeth Bradley Wool colour	Quantity (yards)
1	C1	4
2	C6	17
3	D4	33
4	D5	41
5	D6	19
6	D7	24
7	D11	12
8	E6	16
9	E9	12
10	G9	11
11	I6	19
12	I7	10
13	J9	140

I love sunflowers but I cannot grow them. They need lots of space and a very rich diet; the space I do not have in my garden and the roses seem to get most of the available food. The sunflowers that acted as models for this design were growing in a field in France. When the ultimate sunflower field had eventually been located, I walked in among the giant flowers and found them buzzing with huge lazy bumble bees. In spite of the bees, the sunflowers behaved perfectly, standing motionless in the hot sun to be photographed.

> The swarthy bee is a buccaneer,
> A burly velveted rover,
> Who loves the booming wind in his ear,
> As he sails the seas of clover . . .
> He looks like a gentleman, lives like a lord,
> And works like a Trojan Hero;
> Then loafs all winter upon his hoard,
> With the mercury at zero.

"A more ancient Mariner", Bliss Carman

The Sunflower Circle Design

This sunflower chart complete with bumble bees can be used to make either circular or square pieces of needlework. The background area is painted dark green. In a circular area immediately around the flower a small dot has been added to each square.

If making a flower circle: work the dotted squares only.

If a square is required, ignore the dots and work the whole of the area between the sunflower and the narrow outside border with the same dark green wool (J9).

The square cushion in the photograph on pages 48-9 has two shades of green in the background area. The dotted circular area is worked in olive green (I9) and the rest of the background in the normal (J9). This dual-coloured background was, in fact, worked in error but it was, I feel, fortuitous as it looks most attractive.

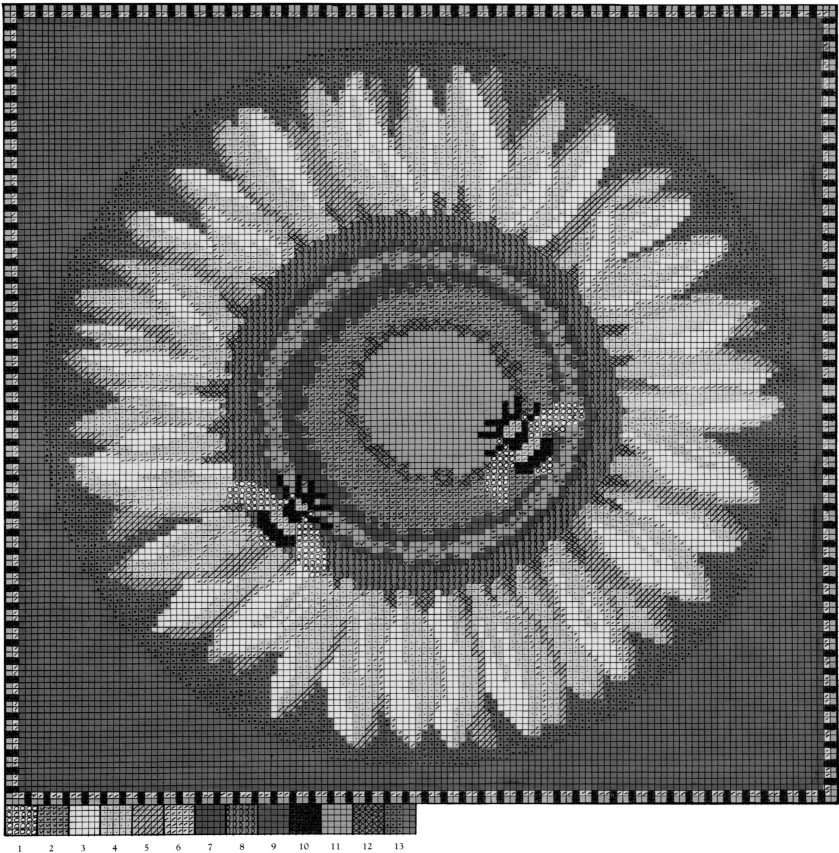

1 2 3 4 5 6 7 8 9 10 11 12 13

SUMMER

Poppy Circle

Poppies are truly antique flowers. Revered and made sacred by the Egyptians, they appear in tomb paintings, jewellery and early medical papyri. The Greeks dedicated the flower to Nyx the goddess of the night and to Morpheus the god of dreams because of its narcotic powers which "lull pain and bring forgetfulness of sorrow". The seed capsule of the opium poppy, the white *Papaver somniferum*, appears frequently in Egyptian, Greek and Roman art. It is invariably shown incized, indicating that the latex containing the opiate has been removed.

Opium in various forms was and still is used as a narcotic over a large part of the globe. Its use was so widespread in nineteenth-century Europe that no stigma was attached to it. Elizabeth Barrett Browning, Coleridge, Keats and Berlioz are only a few of the poets, writers and composers who were addicted to the opium that lurked in laudanum, a

tincture that was widely prescribed as a sleeping draught and general panacea at this time. It was particularly favoured by women, and 1 in 400 middle class, American women were reported to be addicted before its harmful effects were realized. It is difficult to believe that as late as 1898 heroin was advocated as "the perfect drug", "more potent, less harmful and non addicting", in comparison with morphine whose addictive qualities had already been realized. Both drugs come from the poppy.

Wild European poppies, *Papaver rhoeas*, are red. They grow in cornfields and on newly disturbed earth, as was found on battle fields and bombsites in both world wars. The well-known lines by Colonel McCrae are still poignant. He died of wounds in 1918.

> In Flanders' fields the poppies blow
> Between the crosses, row on row,
> That mark our place: and in the sky
> The larks, still bravely singing, fly
> Scarce heard amid the guns below.

The Poppy Circle

The poppy in this design is the oriental poppy *Papaver orientale* which grows wild in Turkey and other eastern Mediterranean countries. Amos Perry is the name most associated with this variety of poppy. In his Hardy Plant Farm at Enfield he developed splendid award-winning varieties in all sorts of colours. They were more compact plants than the wild form with much stronger and more upstanding stems.

In my garden, I grow "Goliath", a tall, strong, blood red poppy. If one only has room for one variety then for me it must be red; poppies in the mind's eye are always red.

> . . . And crush-silk poppies aflash,
> The blood-gush blade-gash
> Flame-rash rudred
> Bud shelling or broad-shed
> Tatter-tassel-tangled and dingle-a-dangled
> Dandy-hung dainty head.

A description of red field poppies from "The Woodlark", Gerard Manley Hopkins (1844-89)

Wool colours and quantities

The quantities listed below are the numbers of yards of Elizabeth Bradley Wool needed to work a square piece with a border as seen on the chart to the right. It measures 86 stitches by 86 stitches and has been worked on 10 mesh interlock canvas using cross stitch.

Colours used: 11 colours including 1 background colour.

The background colour of all the pieces shown in this book is purple (N4).

Number on Chart key	Elizabeth Bradley Wool colour	Quantity (yards)
1	A6	2
2	B9	23
3	B10	28
4	B11	11
5	G11	6
6	H5	3
7	I7	7
8	I10	1
9	N1	2
10	N3	5
11	N4	74

Key number 11 is the background colour, purple (N4). N4 is also used in the design.

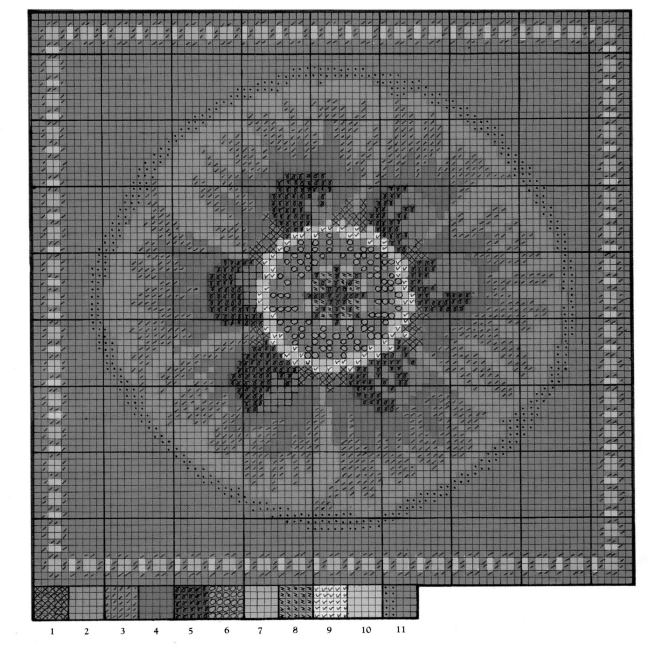

1   2   3   4   5   6   7   8   9   10   11

SUMMER

Pansy Circle

Spring is the time of violets and the small, native and utterly charming *Viola tricolor*, heartsease or love-in-idleness, the oldest and to me, one of the sweetest of the violas.

Autumn brings nurseries full of plain coloured, bright and fresh winter-flowering pansies. I buy them every autumn and they surprise me each year in early spring with the sheer exuberance of their flowering, it seems such an unnatural time of year for pansies to flower.

Summer is when right-minded pansies should be flowering and summer pansies are real characters. The only criteria I insist upon before they are allowed space in the garden is that they must have good faces or blotches as they are properly known. I like to see their round cheerful flowers peering

out from the massive green of the summer garden or sprawling over paths with folded buds modestly bowed and wide open faces raised to the sun.

> . . . Bring the rathe Primrose that forsaken dies.
> The tufted Crow-toe, and pale Gessamine,
> The white Pink and the Pansie freakt with jet,
> The glowing Violet.
> The Musk-rose, and the well attir'd Woodbine.
> With Cowslips wan that hang the pensive hed,
> And every flower that sad embroidery wears.
>
> *Lycidas*, John Milton (1637)

It is difficult to buy separate seed for any but a few named varieties of pansies and generally to get a good selection of faces it is best to grow packets of mixed seed and see what comes up. Swiss Giants Mixed and Tutti Frutti Mixed both give good results, while Super Chalons Giant mixed seed produces pansies with distinctive ruffled and laced petals as well as good, bold blotches. The tawny specimen shown on the chart opposite could have come from any of these packets of seeds.

The flower has been set against a sapphire blue background and edged with a narrow zigzag border to make a pansy square. Two finished pieces were made using the chart opposite. One was sewn with the border and a sapphire blue (M3) background and the other without the border against a dark navy blue (M8) background. The dots on the blue squares of the background of the chart indicate the area that should be stitched to make a pansy circle.

If a tawny pansy does not appeal, use the basic pansy pattern but change the colours to those that you prefer. Any good seed catalogue should provide plenty of ideas for improved versions.

Wool colours and quantities

The quantities listed below are the numbers of yards of Elizabeth Bradley Wool needed to work a square piece with a border as seen on the chart to the right. It measures 80 stitches by 80 stitches and has been worked on 10 mesh interlock canvas using cross stitch.

Colours used: 10 colours including 1 background colour.

The background colours of the pieces shown on page 61 are sapphire blue (M3) and navy blue (M8).

Number on Chart key	Elizabeth Bradley Wool colour	Quantity (yards)
1	C6	19
2	C7	3
3	C11	13
4	D5	9
5	D7	11
6	E6	13
7	I6	4
8	J7	3
9	M3	60
10	M11	4

Key number 9 is the background colour, sapphire blue (M3).

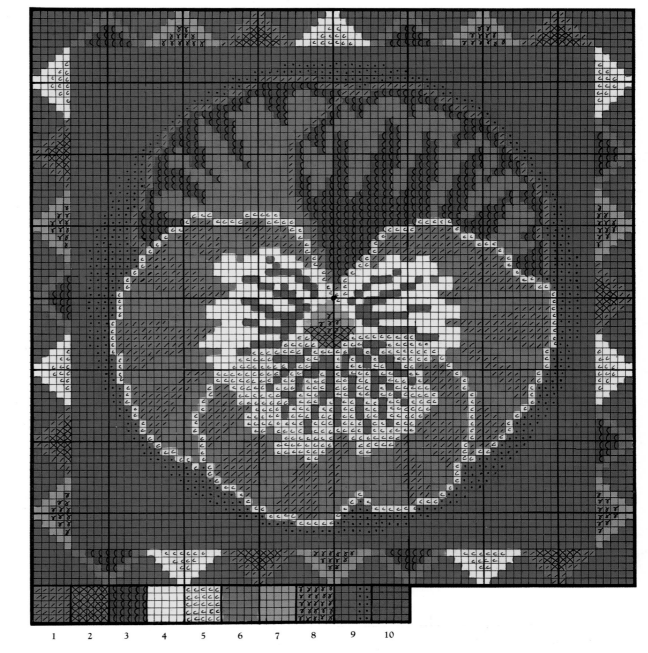

SUMMER

The Sunflower Border

The Sunflower, says Darwin,
Climbs the upland lawn,
And bows in homage to the
rising dawn!
Imbibes with eagle eye the
golden ray,
And watches as it moves the
orb of day.

Erasmus Darwin (1731-1802)

There is a fine description of a sunflower in Gerard's *Herbal*: "The Indian Sun, or the golden floure of Peru, is a plant of such stature and tal-nesse, that in one summer, beeing sowne of a seed in Aprill, it hath risen up to the height of four-teene foot in my garden, where one floure was in weight three pound and two ounces, and crosse overthwart the floure by measure sixteen inches broad. The stalks are upright and straight, of the bignesse of a strong mans arme, beset with large leaves even to the top . . . this great floure is in shape like to the Camomil floure, beset round about with a pale or border of goodly yellow leaves, . . . the middle part whereof is made as it were of unshorn velvet, or some curious cloath wrought with the needle . . . when the plant groweth to maturitie the floures fall away, in place whereof appeareth the seed, black and large, much like the seed of Gourds, set as though a cunning workman had of purpose placed them in very good order, much like the hony-combs of Bees.

"These plants grow of themselves without set-ting or sowing, in Peru, and in divers other pro-vinces of America, from whence the seeds have beene brought into these parts of Europ. There hath bin seen in Spain and other hot regions a plant sowne and nourished up from seed, to attaine to the height of 24 foot in one yeare."

Anyone who has driven through France in July cannot fail to be impressed by the rolling fields of bright yellow sunflowers that stretch to the horizon on either side of the road. Each plant grows from about 6 to 10ft (2 to 3m) tall and the round flowers can be as much as 1ft (30cms) across. The flowers are supposed to follow the path of the sun, turning their heads to follow its path as it moves across the sky from the east where it rises to the west where it sinks below the horizon at dusk. I have watched them but have never managed to observe this phenomenon, yet the belief persists.

Sunflowers are grown for the oil in their black and white striped seeds but they have also become very popular as cut flowers. They will keep for a long time if their ends are dipped in boiling water after they are cut. The half-opened flowers also dry well when hung upside down in the hot sun.

Historic Sunflowers

The generic name *Helianthus annus* is derived from two Greek words helios, the sun and anthos, flower, hence the name sunflower. The flower was the emblem of the Sun God of the Incas and appears carved on their temples. When conse-crated to the gods, Inca virgins wore sunflower crowns made of pure gold on their heads and had sunflowers woven in gold thread on their clothing. Sunflower seeds were placed on the graves of the dead by the North American Indians to sustain them on their journey to the happy hunting grounds and it is the state flower of Kansas. It was a favourite flower of Art Nouveau artists and Van Gogh's painting of the flowers is known world-wide; it fetched the highest price ever for a paint-ing when it was sold at auction in the 1980s.

Sunflower cushions and long borders worked on cream backgrounds. Such borders make decorative bell pulls, pelmets or edgings for curtains or tablecovers. The pale blue of the bedroom is an unusual and pretty combination with the soft yellow of the embroidered sunflowers.

B

C

C

Provençal centre cushion with geometric edging

The quantities listed below are the numbers of yards of Elizabeth Bradley Wool needed to work a square measuring 172 stitches by 172 stitches on 10 mesh interlock canvas using cross stitch.

Number on Chart key	Elizabeth Bradley Wool colour	Quantity (yards)
1	D4	133
4	D7	137
5	E9	27
6	G9	25
11	J8	15

Background quantity for a piece measuring 172 stitches by 172 stitches: 280 yards.

Wool colours and quantities – Sunflower Border strip with geometric edging

The quantities listed below are the numbers of yards of Elizabeth Bradley Wool needed to work a piece measuring 92 stitches by 480 stitches on 10 mesh interlock canvas using cross stitch.

Colours used:
11 plus 1 background colour.

The background colour used on all the pieces in this book is cream (F3).

Number on Chart key	Elizabeth Bradley Wool colour	Quantity (yards)
1	D4	100
2	D5	111
3	D6	60
4	D7	33
5	E9	33
6	G9	33
7	I4	26
8	I10	20
9	J6	80
10	J11	49
11	J8	63

Background quantity for a piece measuring 92 stitches by 480 stitches: 230 yards.

Sunflower Border cushion with Provençal centre

The quantities listed below are the numbers of yards of Elizabeth Bradley Wool needed to work a square measuring 240 stitches by 240 stitches on 10 mesh interlock canvas using cross stitch.

Number on Chart key	Elizabeth Bradley Wool colour	Quantity (yards)
1	D4	104
2	D5	162
3	D6	79
4	D7	61
5	–	–
6	G9	42
7	I4	40
8	I10	27
9	J6	115
10	J11	82
11	J8	67

Background quantity for a piece measuring 240 stitches by 240 stitches: 380 yards.

C	B	D
B	provençal centre	B
D	B	C

ABOVE: *A diagram showing how each unit in the Sunflower Border cushion is arranged.*

This cushion piece was made by using the elements B, C and D together with an area of abstract, spotted pattern in the centre. The background colour is cream (F3).

A Sunflower Border

The Sunflower Border design on pages 70-1 is based on an early nineteenth-century Berlin wool-work chart by my favourite designer A Philipson. In her book *The Art of Needlework* (published in 1840), the Countess of Wilton tells us that "in 1804 a print seller in Berlin named Philipson published a hand-coloured design on checkered paper for needlework." In *The Handbook of Needlework* (published in 1843) Miss Lambert gave the date as 1805 and added that the patterns were "badly executed and devoid of taste".

I have to admit that Philipson's charts are not as well painted as those of some other designers, such as the better known LW Wittich. Probably this is because he used thinner paint which tended to run over the edges of the little squares, and a much more porous and lower-quality paper than his competitors. Certainly, far more Wittich charts were worked than those by Philipson and many more have survived in collections of Berlin woolwork designs. One can only assume from this that

Philipson was less successful than his contemporary, maybe this was because he was ahead of his time – he was certainly more stylish and much less sentimental than other designers of the period. His sunflower design suits the 1990s very well indeed and it is hard to believe that the basic pattern was first published nearly 200 years ago.

Making up the Border

Philipson's original design consisted of three sunflowers in a row with part of a geometric border and a zigzag edging next to it. The two sunflowers at the ends of the line of three were the same, with the one in the middle being different. The basic pattern is therefore composed of two sunflower elements to be called A and B which connect together alternately so that long rows of sunflowers can be worked. Such strips of sunflowers can be used to make bell pulls, pelmets or edgings for curtains. They can be worked with or without the narrow geometric edging.

To make such a pattern turn corners proved complicated and meant that two additional elements of sunflower pattern had to be added to act as corners, these to be called C and D. The easiest way to understand how to use this border is to study the charts on pages 70-1 and the plan above left, together with the photograph of the finished piece to the left. If a larger square or rectangle is required, the additional elements can be added as necessary. The corners remain the same.

All the pieces made with The Sunflower Border in this book have been worked on a cream background (F3). As an alternative, a black (G11) background would be dramatic and I also think the design would work well against a bright brick red (B10) background.

The colours used for my stitched sunflower petals are quite muted compared to those of real flowers; authentic bright yellows would not suit many houses. If, however, you have decorated your home in bright primary shades, then I hope you will work brilliant yellow sunflowers to match. Four shades of bright, rather than muted, yellow wool would be needed.

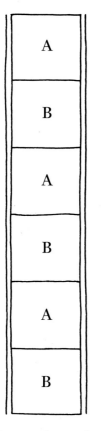

ABOVE: *This strip of six sunflowers was made by alternating the elements A and B.*

The Provençal Centre Design

For me, The Sunflower Border design has a distinct French flavour and reminds me both of the Provençal fabrics that are so popular at the moment and of the stunning, printed cotton textiles that were produced in France during the early nineteenth century. These were known as Provincial patterns after the brightly coloured and gaily patterned cotton prints that were part of the traditional costume in hot and sunny Provence. The production of these fabrics marked the start of a large-scale industry in France. They were the bread and butter product of the mill at Jouy which is better known for the manufacture of the copper-plate printed scenic toiles called Toiles de Jouy. Napoleon is supposed to have visited the factory and told the owner, M. Oberkampf, "You and I wage good war on the English, you by your industry and I by my armies. But your way is the more effective."

A square cotton scarf was part of the Provençal costume. It generally had a small-scale motif in the centre, or field, with a wide and elaborate border around the edge. These borders were also printed separately and then cut into strips so that they could be attached as edgings to lengths of plainer cloth. It seemed an interesting idea to try something similar in needlework and so I painted a small-scale centre pattern. It can be worked on its own or used as the centrepiece of panels made with the more elaborate Sunflower Border.

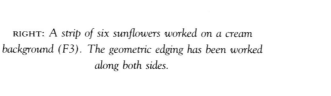

RIGHT: *A strip of six sunflowers worked on a cream background (F3). The geometric edging has been worked along both sides.*

SUMMER

Roses

I heard a rose remark last night,
"It isn't fair it isn't right,
That I should get this
beastly blight."

An incident which clearly shows
That things as lovely as a rose
Have got their troubles, I suppose

Green Fingers Again, Reginald Arkell

"What a pother have authors made with Roses! What a racket have they kept? I shall add, red Roses are under Jupiter, Damask under Venus, White under the Moon, and Provence under the King of France . . . To write at large of every one of these, would make my book smell too big." Culpeper's *Herbal*.

When writing about roses it is difficult not to agree with Culpeper; it is not so much a matter of searching for information about the flower as of sifting through the vast amount of literature and lore surrounding it. It would be a relatively simple matter to fill every page of this book with fascinating facts and fancies about roses, and there are so many varieties that one could happily fill a book with nothing but rose designs. However, this is not purely a rose book and though needlewomen seem to love embroidering them they enjoy portraying other flowers too and so the number of designs has been limited to two. Both are distinctly Victorian and romantic in style.

The rose has been widely fêted in literature and lore because of its ephemeral and luscious beauty, its scent and its part in the history of many countries. It would be impossible to cover the subject at all comprehensively with Shakespeare alone mentioning roses more than 70 times in plays and sonnets. Likewise, a whole treatise could be written on rose recipes and remedies pertaining to roses. After much sifting and sad expunging, these pages hold a mixture of snippets and poems that I found interesting and appealing.

The rose is generally associated with beauty and love but also with a certain sadness and regret at the inevitable passing of youth and loveliness. It is also the flower of secrecy and silence, hence the expression, Sub Rosa – under the rose, to mean a solemn pledge of secrecy. Many poems to roses were written before the advent of perpetual flowering species, roses bloomed in mid-summer and were gone for another year. The tight buds full of promise opened into many-petalled flowers of almost incredible perfection, these inevitably became faded and overblown and then withered and died. The flowering of roses was a poignant annual reminder of the preciousness of youth in centuries when it was all too short.

Gather ye rosebuds while ye may,
Old Time is still a-flying:
And this same flower that smiles to-day,
To-morrow will be dying.

"To the Virgins, to make much of Time",
Robert Herrick (1591-1674)

The Origin of the Rose

Many myths exist suggesting possible origins of the rose. The Roman one is, as usual, succinct and charming. They believed that the rose sprung from Venus's rosy blushes when she was spied in the nude by Jupiter. She gave the new flower to Cupid, her son, who in turn gave it to Harpocrates, the God of silence. The gift was made to induce Harpocrates to keep silent about any scandalous happenings up on Mount Olympus. This all seems quite reasonable and much more cheerful than some of the flights of fancy from other countries and times. Jewish folklore, for instance, changed flames into roses before they could burn an innocent girl to death and American stories constantly tell of women being turned into roses as they are murdered. The white Cherokee Rose and the red, nasty smelling, Grant Rose both apparently arose in this rather grisly fashion.

Then, then, in strange eventful hour,
The earth produced an infant flower,
Which sprung with blushing tinctures drest,
And wantoned o'er its parent's breast.
The gods beheld this brilliant birth,
And hailed the Rose, the boon of earth.

Part of a poem on the origin of the rose by the Roman poet, Anacreon (*c.* 572-488 BC).

The Romans seem to have really enjoyed their roses which to them signified joy and pleasure as well as beauty. They were less sentimental about them than we are and used rose flowers and petals to help celebrate all sorts of bacchanalian revels and festivals. Swags of roses were used to decorate

O Rose, thou art sick
The invisible worm,
That flies in the night,
In the howling storm,

Has found out thy bed
Of crimson joy;
And his dark secret love
Does thy life destroy.

"The Sick Rose", William Blake
(1757-1827)

boxes at the games and rosy wreaths to adorn the brows of the winners. Romans sat on seats in litters covered with rose petals and even slept on beds of rose petals, hence the expression "It's not a bed of roses". Rose garlands, petals and chaplets were essential dinner party decorations and Cleopatra covered the floor of her banqueting hall with an 18-inch (45-cm) deep layer of rose petals when Anthony came to dine. The emperor Elagabalus managed to actually kill several of his supper guests by showering them with so many rose petals that they suffocated.

Echoes of the rose's disreputable and pagan past clung for a long time afterwards. It was not until the Middle Ages that the flower became respectable again and the Virgin Mary was named "the rose without thorns". Rosaries are used to count prayers to Our Lady and were made originally from pressed rose petals which gave off scent as the beads were said; this was supposed to remind the prayer of the roses in Mary's garden. The concept of building beautiful round windows in the shape of roses was brought back from the Holy Land by the crusaders. Under the magnificent example at York Minster is written "as the rose is the flower of all flowers this is the house of all houses."

The rose is the national flower of England and stories about it are associated with many kings and queens. The striped rose, *Rosa mundi*, was named after Fair Rosamond the mistress of Henry II. Although their love story and the rose bower that the king made for her, were immortalized in ballads and poems she was, in fact, very unpopular with the people and the inscription carved on her tomb was not complimentary: "Here rose the graced, not rose the chaste, reposes; The scent that rises is no scent of roses."

Rose Associations

The rose became England's national emblem during the Wars of the Roses in the fifteenth century. The Lancastrians wore the red apothecary's rose, *Rosa gallica officinalis*, while the Yorkists

adopted the white, *Rosa alba-sempervirens*, as their badge. The Tudor rose has both red and white petals to symbolize the union of the York and Lancaster factions in the marriage of Henry Tudor to Elizabeth of York. The Jacobites who needed to work in secret in an attempt to get the Stuarts restored to the throne took the white rose, *Rosa alba maxima*, as their emblem.

France too, has strong associations with the rose. The empress Josephine adored them and planted over 250 varieties in her garden at Malmaison. Although her garden is now in ruins, all her roses and many more can be seen in the world famous rose garden called the Roseraie de l'Hay. Redouté, the great flower portraitist, was of course French; he was commissioned by Josephine to paint her roses and his book of engravings *Les Roses* must still be the best known rose book in the world.

Many of the best modern roses were developed in America and several states have adopted roses as their emblem. New York state is one such and Georgia, with the white Cherokee rose, another. Iowa took a wild rose as its emblem while the district of Columbia is associated with the American Beauty Rose as is Dakota with the Prairie Rose.

OVERLEAF: *Roses and lace have always been associated with weddings and romance. The cushions and stool covers made from the Roses and Lace design on page 79 make perfect accessories for this bridal morning scene.*

SUMMER

Roses and Lace

Wool colours and quantities

The quantities listed below are the numbers of yards of Elizabeth Bradley Wool needed to work a piece measuring 125 stitches by 125 stitches on 10 mesh interlock canvas using cross stitch.

· Colours used:
24 including background colours.

The background colours shown in the pieces on pages 76-7 are cream (F3) and lemon yellow (D2) on the small round stool, cream (F3) and aquamarine (K8) on the larger stool, and on the right-hand cushion, and cream (F3) and pale blue (M4) and cream (F3) and lilac (N5) on the two left-hand cushions.

Number on Chart key	Elizabeth Bradley Wool colour	Quantity (yards)
1	A2	13
2	A3	11
3	A4	17
4	A5	10
5	A6	7
6	F5	7
7	B2	9
8	B3	12
9	D11	3
10	F9	7
11	F11	8
12	F3	58
13	H6	17
14	H7	14
15	I1	5
16	I4	11
17	I7	5
18	J4	7
19	J5	7
20	J6	13
21	J7	10
22	J8	7
23	J9	9
24	K8	80

Key numbers 12 and 24 are the background colours, cream (F3) and aquamarine (K8).

The rose is the queen of the flowers and roses are the world's most popular cut flower. A red rose signifies love and sending a bunch of red roses to a woman is still a sign of admiration and regard throughout the western world. In the past, different coloured roses conveyed a variety of messages and in *The Language of Flowers* there are 34 different roses, each with its own meaning. Most of these meanings are positive and romantic but a few are quite contradictory and contrary so care had to be taken when choosing a corsage or gift of roses. A yellow rose, for instance, indicated a decrease in love and jealousy. The hundred-leaved rose, *Rosa centifolia*, meant pride and the china rose, *Rosa chinensis*, conveyed the rather insulting message that beauty was your only attraction. The cabbage rose was the uncomplicated ambassador of love and perhaps this is why it was so popular on lacy, Victorian Valentines and in the woolwork embroideries of the nineteenth century.

> The maidens came
> When I was in my mother's bower;
> I had all that I would.
> The bailey beareth the bell away;
> The lily, the rose, the rose I lay.
>
> The silver is white, red is the gold;
> The robes they lay in fold.
> The bailey beareth the lull away;
> The lily, the rose, the rose I lay.
>
> And thro the glass window shines the sun.
> How should I love, and I so young?
> The bailey beareth the lull away;
> The lily, the rose, the rose I lay.

"Bridal Morning", Anon (fifteenth–sixteenth century)

Weddings reach their peak in mid-summer every year, the weather tends to be at its best and so it is an obvious time of year to choose. It is also the time when almost every variety of rose is in flower. It is not surprising perhaps that over the centuries weddings, roses and romance have become inextricably entwined.

> I sent a message by the Rose
> That words could not convey;
> Sweet vows I never dared to breathe,
> And wishes pure as they;
> A mute but tell-tale messenger,
> It could not do me wrong;
> But told the passion I concealed,
> And hopes I cherished long.
>
> My Love received it with a smile,
> She read its thought and sighed,
> Then placed it on her happy breast,
> And wore it till it died.
> Immortal Rose! it could not die:
> The spirit which it bore,
> Lives in her heart as first in mine –
> A joy for evermore.

"The Rose's Errand", C. Mackay

A crown or wreath of roses meant reward of virtue, and as virtue was the pre-requisite of every Victorian bride, marriage was seen as its just reward. Not to get married was regarded as a disgrace and loss of virtue as a total disaster, if having lost it you perished in the snow it served you right. Rosebuds convey messages such as girlhood and pure loveliness and so traditionally came to be used in the wedding bouquet. Rose petals were thrown over the happy couple after the knot was tied.

The Roses and Lace Design

This rose design shows a pair of cabbage roses surrounded by a border of lace. It is a romantic and pretty pattern and so it seemed suitable to work it against a variety of soft, pastel coloured backgrounds. To emphasize the delicate lacy theme, the background colour has been softened with pin stripes worked in cream wool. Like all striped designs this one is best worked on its side so that the stripes are worked along their length rather than across it. A smoother piece of needlework is achieved in this way. The design can be worked with or without the border.

1 2 3 4 5² 6 7 8 9 10 11 12 13 14 15 16 17 18 19 20 21 22 23 24

SUMMER

Rosebaby

Cupid and my Campaspe play'd
At cards for kisses – Cupid paid:
He stakes his quiver, bow,
and arrows,
His mother's doves, and team
of sparrows;
Loses them too; then down
he throws
The coral of his lips, the rose . . .

"Cards and Kisses", John Lyly
(1554-1606)

The Rosebaby emerging from the heart of a red rose is actually Cupid, the Roman god of love, who with his bow and arrow made mischief among mortals by causing them to fall in love, often with the most unlikely and unsuitable people. Cupid was given the newly created rose flower by his mother, Venus, and so was often depicted crowned with a wreath of roses. Representations of the young god frequently appeared in both Hellenistic and Renaissance art where his presence indicated that the theme of a painting was connected with love. Sometimes he appears in pictures of Jupiter who spent much of his time seducing innocent maidens. At other times he is blindfolded to show that love is blind or seen playing with the weapons of war to symbolize that the power of love can disarm the strong. Renaissance painters generally showed him as a winged boy or youth, whereas in later Baroque and Rococo paintings he changes into a chubby baby.

The Rosebaby Design

This rather whimsical design is a great favourite of mine, it is an example of an original and early chart from one of my favourite periods of needlework. It was first published in a booklet of 12 charts called *Neuestes Toilettengeschenk* produced in Leipzig in 1813. I found it in a Flemish book about Berlin woolwork by Josephine Landwehr-Vogels. Berlin woolwork charts produced in the first 30 or

The red rose whispers of passion,
And the white rose breathes of love;
O, the red rose is a falcon,
And the white rose is a dove.
But I send you a cream-white rosebud
With a flush on its petal tips;
For the love that is purest and sweetest
Has a kiss of desire on the lips.

"A White Rose", John Boyle O'Reilly

so years of the nineteenth century are particularly fresh and original whereas later in the century one artist copied another and they tended to become more repetitive and clumsy.

The fat infant and the overblown crimson rose in this early design seem a ridiculous subject to have been attempted in woolwork. If painted in watercolours or even stitched in delicate silks such a subject might have had a chance of attaining real prettiness, as a woolwork design it amuses me. The design, made into a picture or a cushion, makes an unusual christening present for a new baby.

The example overleaf was made for my nephew Joseph Arthur Lillington and his name and the date of his birth were stitched below the picture. The design can be worked with or without an edging. The sky can be sewn in black as shown on the original chart or alternatively stitched in sky blue (L1) or cream (F3) to achieve a lighter effect. The lettering was taken from the alphabet on page 21.

Joseph Arthur Lillington sleeps in the garden. He is surrounded by a selection of Rosebaby cushions and summer flowers. A spray of roses shades him from the sun.

LOUISE ODIER

ROSE RECIPES

ELEANOUR SINCLAIR ROHDE
DECORATED BY
HELEN KAPP

LANGUAGE
OF
FLOWERS

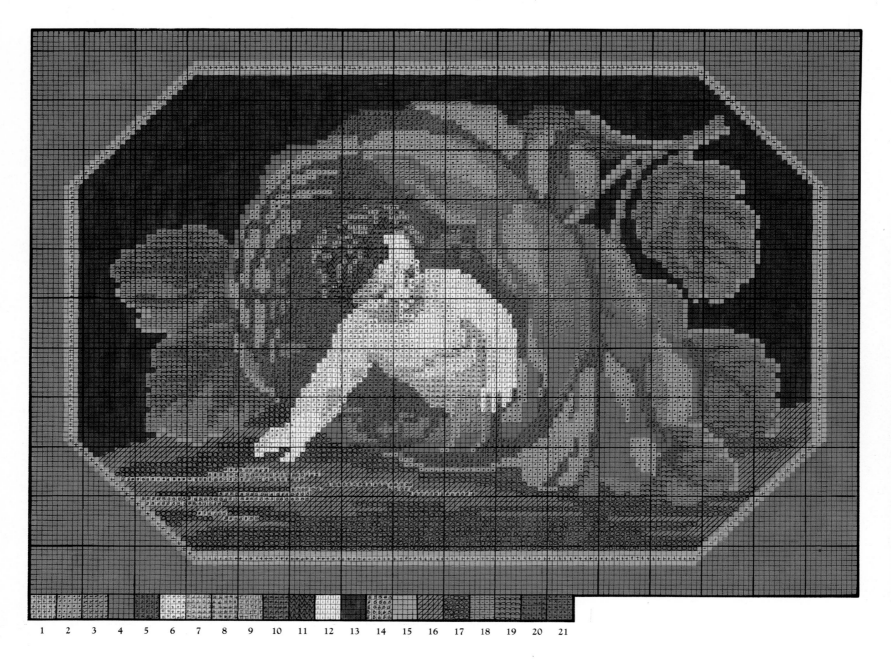

1   2   3   4   5   6   7   8   9   10   11   12   13   14   15   16   17   18   19   20   21

Wool colours and quantities

The quantities listed below are the numbers of yards of Elizabeth Bradley Wool needed to work a piece measuring 160 stitches by 114 stitches on 10 mesh interlock canvas using cross stitch.

Colours used: 21 including
1 background colour

The background colour of the pieces shown on page 81 are crimson (A6) (as shown on the chart opposite), and dark pink (A5). The sky colours of the pieces shown are black (G11) (as shown on the chart), and blue (L1).

Number on Chart key	Elizabeth Bradley Wool colour	Quantity (yards)
1	A3	9
2	A4	25
3	A5	18
4	A6	98
5	A8	24
6	B2	10
7	B3	6
8	B4	4
9	E5	4
10	E7	4
11	E10	3
12	F5	8
13	G11	63
14	I3	7
15	I4	19
16	I8	15
17	I10	26
18	J6	19
19	J7	18
20	J8	9
21	N4	10

Key number 4 is the background colour, crimson (A6). A6 is also used in the design.

Warm summer sun, shine kindly here;
Warm southern wind, blow softly here;
Green sod above, lie light, lie light –
Good-night, dear heart, good-night, good-night.

"Epitaph", Mark Twain (1835-1910),
for the death of his daughter, Olivia.

AUTUMN

AUTUMN

I saw old Autumn in the
misty morn
Stand shadowless like
Silence, listening
To silence, for no lonely
bird would sing
Into his hollow ear from
woods folorn,
Nor lowly hedge nor
solitary thorn;
Shaking his languid locks all
dewy bright
With tangled gossamer that fell
by night,
Pearling his coronet of
golden corn.

"Autumn", Thomas Hood
(1799-1845)

Season of mists and mellow fruitfulness!
Close bosom-friend of the maturing sun;
Conspiring with him how to load and bless
With fruit the vines that round the thatch-eaves
run;
To bend with apples the moss'd cottage-trees,
And fill all fruit with ripeness to the core;
To swell the gourd, and plump the hazel shells
With a sweet kernel; to set budding more
And still more, later flowers for the bees,
Until they think warm days will never cease;
For Summer has o'er brimm'd their clammy cells.

"To Autumn", John Keats (1775-1821)

Keats called autumn the "Season of mists and mellow fruitfulness", it is also the season of mushrooms and toadstools, pungent smells of wet, black earth and fallen leaves, golden leaves and golden light, spiders' webs and dewy mornings. In the garden, the dahlias and Michaelmas daisies are flowering. Chrysanthemums shake their shaggy heads and the scented stars of nicotiana and the pale evening primroses glimmer in the early dusk of the rapidly shortening days. Leaves turn yellow or gold or red, and fall to become dry and crisp and be scuffed and kicked by children's Wellington boots. The branches of pyracantha, berberis and cotoneaster are covered in berries.

For many poets, autumn seems to bring on a melancholy mood but for gardeners it is a busy and very satisfying season. The work done now stays done because the weeds have at last almost stopped sprouting. Each section of the garden can be enjoyed as it is tackled in turn. Herbaceous clumps can be split and favourite plants spread to grow in other flowerbeds. It is a time to put right the mistakes of the previous autumn and move tall plants back and too short ones forward. Whole shrubs

and even quite large trees can be dug up and replanted somewhere else, they are usually quite happy as long as they are well fed and watered.

For the more haphazard gardener, who prefers impromptu propagation, it is a good time to stick long heel cuttings of short-lived shrubs deeply into the damp earth. They can be popped in here and there, wherever it would be handy to have them if they were to survive and grow. Lavender, perennial wallflowers, pinks, hebes and hydrangeas seem quite happy to be propagated in this rather informal fashion.

Autumn plants

If new shrubs and roses were ordered in good time they will start to arrive in November and unless their future homes have been prepared for them well in advance it always seems a rush to get them in before the first frosts. The garden centres are full of spring-flowering bulbs and it is difficult to resist buying just a few more even if there is really no room for them. Autumn-flowering bulbs can bring just as much pleasure and are often forgotten. The autumn-flowering crocus, the colchicum, sends up its strange pale stems topped with lilac flowers in October or November while the slightly earlier-flowering *Nerine bowdenii* from South Africa performs perfectly in dry and inhospitable parts of the garden. Its flowers, like elegant pink agapanthus, are not seen nearly often enough in autumn gardens. Even in a small garden it is worth having a clump of elephant lilies, *Crinum powellii*. Their leaves are spring green all summer and in autumn they produce thick stemmed, handsome lily flowers in deep pink or white.

After gardening for many years it eventually sinks in to the brain of even the most stolid gar-

PREVIOUS PAGE: *Nuts, seed-pods, leaves and fir cones can be used to make enchanting autumn decorations. Once they have been made, nut wreaths last indefinitely and do not fade like some dried flower decorations. Interspersed among the nuts and cones are some fine pieces of eighteenth- and nineteenth-century treen and a variety of small needlework items made from the Wreath of Oakleaves design on page 104.*

dener that feeding and yet more feeding is one of the secrets of having a really thriving garden. Most gardeners nurture a compost heap somewhere in the garden and autumn is a good time to harvest it. Good compost should be moist and black, smell deliciously rich but not nasty and be full of wriggling bright pink worms. If the garden is near the sea, as mine is, then an autumn dressing of seaweed can be very nourishing, but best of all is well-rotted manure. If it is mixed with composted bark it makes the most superb of all soil tonics and mulches.

Autumn Bonfires and Festivals

All the cutting back and clearing that takes place in autumn leaves one with large volumes of woody debris; this is not suitable for composting unless it is well pulverized but it does make superb bonfire fodder. Autumn bonfires are one of the casualties of smokeless zones. Nice clean air is wonderful but it is a real deprivation not to be able to assemble a satisfying heap of garden rubbish and then see it all disappear in one great conflagration complete with billows of smoke and showers of sparks. As the smoke from my last private bonfire nearly asphyxiated many of the inhabitants of Beaumaris I now just go along and admire the huge communal one that burns on the beach each Guy Fawkes night on 5 November instead of having my own.

Halloween, on 31 October, is another fixture in the autumn calendar. Faces are cut into pumpkins and lit from within by a candle. Children dress up and visit the neighbours to receive treats; householders who disappoint them may have tricks played upon them. Trick or treat is an American custom which has been adopted in Britain to be enjoyed along with the more traditional apple bobbing and toffee apples. The fourth Thursday of each November brings another American festival which this time we cannot share, Thanksgiving Day. On this day all the members of a family try to gather together to celebrate the first harvest of the Pilgrim Fathers in 1621. A special dinner of turkey and pumpkin pie is served every year.

A more ancient autumn celebration than Thanksgiving is Harvest Festival when churches all over Britain are decorated with sheaves of corn, harvest loaves and baskets of fruit and vegetables. Pulpits are hung with bunches of grapes and berries, and pew ends and window sills are wreathed with dahlias and chrysanthemums. Huge inedible marrows and great fat pumpkins squat in unlikely corners and thanksgiving is made to God for all the produce of the year.

All things bright and beautiful,
All creatures great and small,
All things wise and wonderful,
The Lord God made them all.

Each little flower that opens,
Each little bird that sings,
He made their glowing colours,
He made their tiny wings.

The purple-headed mountain,
The river running by,
The sunset and the morning,
That brightens up the sky.

The cold wind in the winter,
The pleasant summer sun,
The ripe fruits in the garden,
He made them every one.

The tall trees in the greenwood,
The meadows for our play,
The rushes by the water,
To gather every day.

He gave us eyes to see them,
And lips that we may tell,
How great is God Almighty,
Who has made all things well.

CF Alexander

The Autumn Sampler

Silk colours and quantities

The quantities listed below are the number of skeins of DMC six-stranded perle cotton needed to work a sampler 163 stitches by 163 stitches. Each length of cotton should be split in half and the sampler worked with three strands only.

The sampler shown on page 89 was worked on 100% linen scrim, 91cms wide which has approximately 20 threads to the inch. Each stitch should be worked over two threads.

Number on Chart key	DMC thread number	Number of skeins
1	355	2
2	729	1-2
3	781	2
4	783	2
5	400	1-2
6	834	1-2
7	869	1
8	838	1
9	370	1-2
10	733	1-2
11	3052	1-2
12	3011	1
13	730	2
14	935	1-2
15	580	2-3
16	3362	2
17	927	1
18	926	1
19	3041	1-2
20	327	1

The pagoda on this autumn sampler was based on one found on a sampler by "Sarah Mitton finis'd April 2nd in the year of our Lord 1825." My pagoda stands on the shore of an ornamental lake stocked with large goldfish, a cat waits hopefully on the bank for unwary fish. Around it grow an array of shrubs and small trees that would add interest to any autumn garden. They include fuchsias, agapanthus, maple and apple trees and a bush of orange-red cotoneaster berries.

A border of fruits and flowers surrounds the pagoda. There are purple dahlias at each of the four corners and a cluster of hazelnuts, or filberts, at the centre of each side. In between them are bunches of red berries and orange-yellow rose hips. In the sky, the stars twinkle and the sickle moon shines.

All autumn gardens have their own charm but it is at this time of year that the great landscape gardens of Britain really come into their own. An expanse of rolling parkland looks magnificent in the misty golden light of autumn – water birds gather on ornamental lakes. Trees in shades of russet, ochre and red create patchwork effects on hillsides while cattle and deer stand under stately oaks and chestnuts still draped with their last leaves. The small, charming but useless garden buildings called follies seem an essential part of the hazy view.

If we had the space it would be fun to install a small personal folly in the shape of a pagoda in our garden. We could sit on its top tier and admire the view of the Menai Straits and Snowdonia. Sadly, such a folly might look rather out of place in Beaumaris and I expect that the local planning authorities would not look upon it at all kindly. Our ancestors suffered no such restraints on their fantasies when they built charming and whimsical garden houses in the early eighteenth century.

This was the time when many of the great houses were laying out gardens and parks. A gardening book of the time written by Stephan Switzer and called *Ichnographica Rustica or The Nobleman, Gentleman, and Gardener's Recreation* advised his readers to "endeavor to follow and improve the Advantages of Nature, and not to strain beyond her due bounds." The sort of improvements he had in mind included lakes and temples, groves, mazes and labyrinths all of which fitted into a theoretically natural, but in fact highly idealized, Arcadian landscape. Follies, statues and obelisks were used to add interest and a focal point to many of the vistas and woodland walks that were so fashionable.

Towards the middle of the century, taste changed and the garden landscape became less contrived. In the quotation below, Horace Walpole expresses the general desire for more simplicity, after nearly 50 years of fantasy, gardeners were surfeited not only with folly but also with the building of follies:

> "Men tire of expence that is obvious to few spectators . . . The Doric portico, the Palladian Bridge, the Gothic Ruin, the Chinese Pagoda, that surprise the stranger, soon lose their charms to their surfeited master . . . But the ornament whose merit soonest fades, is the hermitage, or scene adapted to contemplation. It is almost comic to set aside a quarter of one's garden to be melancholy in. Prospect, animated prospect, is the theatre that will always be the most frequented."

Garden styles and ornaments swing in and out of fashion over a period of time. By the nineteenth century there was a new generation of gardeners and with a typical Victorian love of everything ornate they could not resist adding a few follies to their already overcrowded gardens. Many countries provided inspiration: Italy for Palladian temples and grottos, India for exotic glass houses and domes, and Egypt for the occasional pyramid.

The garden and hedgerows are full of fruit, fungi, rosehips and late flowers. It is a rich time of year for both palette and eye. A selection of autumn's bounty has been assembled to frame this seasonal sampler.

Wool colours and quantities

The quantities listed below are the numbers of yards of Elizabeth Bradley Wool needed to work a piece 169 stitches by 169 stitches on 10 mesh interlock canvas using cross stitch.

Colours used:
20 plus 1 background colour.

When working the woolwork below from the chart opposite, the gold line border was omitted and four extra rows of background colour were worked around the edges.

The background colour used in the piece shown on page 2 is black (G11).

Number on Chart key	Elizabeth Bradley Wool colour	Quantity (yards)
1	B10	37
2	C5	22
3	C6	32
4	C7	22
5	C11	24
6	D5	26
7	E7	17
8	G7	38
9	I3	26
10	I4	27
11	I5	26
12	I7	17
13	I10	43
14	I11	30
15	J6	46
16	J8	34
17	L1	6
18	L3	22
19	M10	28
20	N11	28

Background quantity for a piece measuring 169 stitches by 169 stitches: 180 yards.

The Origin of Pagodas

Pagodas are popularly supposed to come from China, in fact they are far more characteristic of Burma where they stand on every hillside and in most villages. They are erected by pious Buddhists in order to gain merit. Their shape is supposed to be based on the most beautiful shape known to man, the female breast. Over the years, the shape has been modified so that now most pagodas have tapering roofs crowned with a spire. From the roofs hang dangling strings of metal and glass objects which tinkle in the breeze.

Chinese pagodas have many tiers and their presence in British gardens reflects the eighteenth-century vogue for chinoiserie. The liking for things Chinese has never really left us and "Chinese Chippendale" bridges and garden seats are still a popular feature in modern gardens. The first garden building in the oriental style was built in the Elysian fields at Stowe in 1738 while the best-known pagoda is the Great Pagoda at Kew Gardens built in 1761. It is an immitation of the Chinese Taa, described in an account of the *Buildings, Gardens etc of the Chinese* by William Chambers in 1757. There is another pagoda at Alton Towers, a Chinese garden and an Egyptian garden at Biddulph Grange, and a Chinese aviary at Dropmore in Buckinghamshire.

"To know all the different scenes which may be introduced in a pleasure-ground in modern times, it is only necessary to visit such a place as Alton Towers, in Staffordshire, where . . . may be seen pagodas, hermitages, an imitation of Stonehenge, and of other Druidical monuments, shellwork, gilt domes, and huge blocks of mossy rock, bridges, viaducts and many other curious objects."

The Ladies Companion to the Flower Garden,
Mrs Loudon (1841)

1 2 3 4 5 6 7 8 9 10 11 12 13 14 15 16 17 18 19 20

AUTUMN

The Nasturtium and Butterfly Border

And gay nasturtium writhing
up a fence
Splotching with mock sunlight
sunless days
When latening summer brings
the usual mist

"The Garden", Vita Sackville-West
(1892-1962)

Nasturtiums flower from mid-summer right through to the frosts of late autumn. When the first delicate flush of summer is long gone and the beds are looking tired and dispirited, it is a pleasure to welcome the fresh, flame-coloured flowers of the nasturtium. If, sitting, surveying your garden one evening you notice sparks coming from your nasturtium flowers then do not think you have serious eyesight or mental problems. You will not be the first to witness this phenomenon and, in fact, you will be in distinguished company for not only the daughter of the botanist, Linnaeus, but also the poet and novelist, Goethe, both reported such an occurrence at the end of the eighteenth century. The sparking is apparently due to the high phosphoric acid content of the flowers.

Although nasturtiums are annuals they will seed themselves and then come up year after year all over the garden. They are tough, uncomplaining plants that will grow almost anywhere and are quite happy to meander and sprawl wherever they are needed in the most obliging way. By early autumn, climbing varieties will have totally covered fences, trellis, unsightly banks, or rubbish heaps with their round, blue-green leaves and bright flowers. Even the least green-fingered person in the world could grow nasturtiums and they are perfect as seeds for children to plant as they are almost guaranteed to come up and will then sprout and grow almost as fast as Jack's beanstalk.

Nasturtiums originated in South America and were introduced to Britain via Spain and France in the late sixteenth century. The creeping variety, *Tropaelum majus*, arrived in 1597 followed by the climbing variety from Peru in 1684. Gerard must have been one of the first gardeners in Britain to grow the nasturtium. His splendid description of the plant in the 1636 edition of his herbal expresses a certain wonder at the ways of a new and unusual plant.

"Cresses of India have many weake and feeble branches, rising immediatly from the ground, dispersing themselves far abroad; by meanes whereof one plant doth occupie a great circuit of ground, as doth the great Bindeweede.

The tender stalks divide themselves into sundry branches, trailing likewise upon the ground, somewhat bunched or swollen up at every joint or knee . . . The leaves are round . . . the foot-stalke of the leafe commeth forth on the backeside almost in the middest of the leafe . . . The flours are dispersed throughout the whole plant, of colour yellow, with a crossed star overthwart the inside, of a deep Orange color: unto the backe-part of the same doth hang a taile or spurre . . . The seeds of this rare and faire plant came from the Indies into Spaine . . . This beautifull Plant is called in Latine, Nasturtium Indicum: in English, Indian Cresses . . . We have no certaine knowledge of his nature and vertues . . . "

As can be seen in this description, the plant was originally given the same generic name as water-cress, *Nasturtium officinale*, because it had a similar peppery taste. The name nasturtium is from the Latin *nasus tortus*, distorted nose, perhaps the aromatic juices and pungent smell caused the nose of the classifier to wrinkle up in distaste. Although the generic name was later changed to tropaelum the term nasturtium stuck and it is still used as the common everyday name for the plant. The name tropaelum was derived from the Greek, *tropaion*, which was a pillar set up on a battlefield on which captured armour is hung. The round leaf was supposed to resemble a shield and the flower a blood-stained, burnished, golden Greek helmet. The obscurity of this reasoning shows once again how vital a classical education is to any self-respecting botanist. Both the flowers and the leaves of nasturtiums can be put in salads to add colour and to give a peppery piquant taste. The green seed pods also taste "hot" and can be pickled and used like capers. Dried and powdered, they can be used as a mustard. The juices of the plant were supposed by herbalists to "purge the brain and quicken the

spirit". Being high in Vitamin C they certainly helped to ward off scurvy. In the language of flowers, a nasturtium stands for patriotism.

Nasturtiums come in all the flaming colours of autumn. Bright red and orange, yellow and cream, crimson and scarlet. Seeds are available by variety and in mixed packets. Every year I plant seeds of Alaska Mixed because it has variegated leaves in which the green is charmingly splashed and dappled with cream. "Peach Melba" has flowers the colour of clotted cream and "Cherry Rose", an old variety, has soft crimson flowers. I have yet to grow "Indian Chief" with purple-tinted leaves and semi-double scarlet flowers, it sounds an interesting variety to try next year.

If, as well as flowers, you like butterflies in your garden then nasturtiums are good plants to grow. Cabbage white butterflies in particular like to lay their eggs on the leaves and with nasturtium plants producing these so fast there is no danger of whole plants being eaten.

Nasturtiums and Butterflies

This nasturtium border should, strictly speaking, feature at least one cabbage white butterfly but, in fact, does not as the pale colour of its wings would have stood out too much from the other autumnal colours in the design. Instead, there is a selection of other species that are reasonably common visitors to many late summer and autumn gardens.

Fluttering around the corner section of the border are a clouded yellow, a peacock and a grizzled skipper. A small tortoiseshell butterfly joins together the various sections of the border, and a purple hairstreak and a painted lady butterfly can be found among the round nasturtium leaves and brilliantly-coloured flowers and buds on the side sections. If you look carefully, you will also find two wasps and several caterpillars.

Nasturtiums sometimes occur on Berlin woolwork charts among other flowers but rarely on their own; they are usually just one of several flowers in a mixed border or arrangement. A highly unusual chart by "Bruno Borner in Berlin" which features nasturtiums only was lent to me by Brenda Bean who lives in Charlotte, Carolina. It was a great help with the painting of this border as the structure and character of a nasturtium flower is not the easiest thing to express in stitches. Another designer's method of resolving the problem can save an awful lot of trial and error.

The Nasturtium Border

This border is designed to edge squares of needlework that measure 160 stitches by 160 stitches. The carpet on page 101 has been made with six central squares. The Pansy, The Lily and The Cyclamen can be worked from the charts in this book or as kits. The Auricula is available as a kit only and The Christmas Rose and The Iris can only be worked from the charts in this book.

The central squares of such a carpet are made separately and then sewn together and edged with the border. The pieces are joined by overlapping the edges of the canvases and then stitching through them both. Joints made in this way are both strong and neat.

Many nineteenth-century carpets were made using the same principle. It was far more practical for Victorian ladies to sew the various parts of a carpet separately and then stitch them together at the end than it was to make a carpet in one large piece. At that time, Berlin woolwork was not only an all-consuming hobby but also a social pastime. Pieces of work were either taken out in a workbag to stitch and display, when making calls on other ladies or they were set up on a frame in the drawing room in the evening.

—————

OVERLEAF: *Baskets of nasturtiums arranged with other autumnal flowers and fruit and photographed against a wall of bright crimson Virginia creeper. The Nasturtium and Butterfly Border around the carpet and in the trug on the table was worked from the charts on pages 96 and 97.*

THIS PAGE AND OPPOSITE: *Two rows of squares have been left blank on both of these charts. The blank squares that occur between the outer two rows, yellow ochre (C6) and grass green (J6), and the four rows of darker green (J8), are to indicate a delay in working. The two outermost rows are worked together after the carpet has been joined together (see instructions on page 99).*

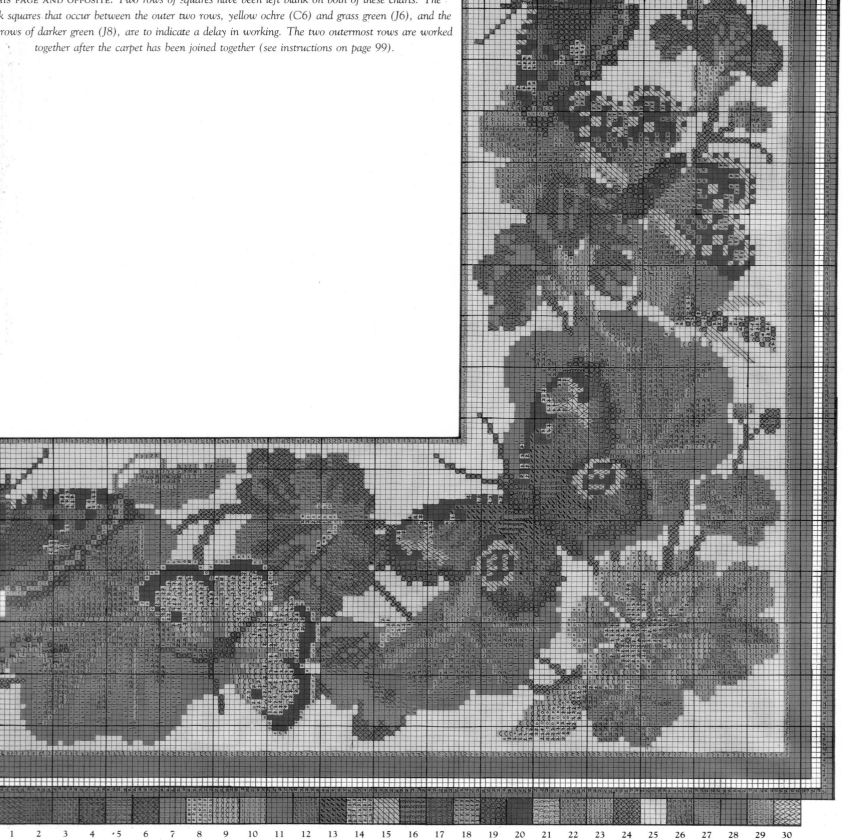

1 2 3 4 5 6 7 8 9 10 11 12 13 14 15 16 17 18 19 20 21 22 23 24 25 26 27 28 29 30

NEEDLEWORK ANTIQUE FLOWERS

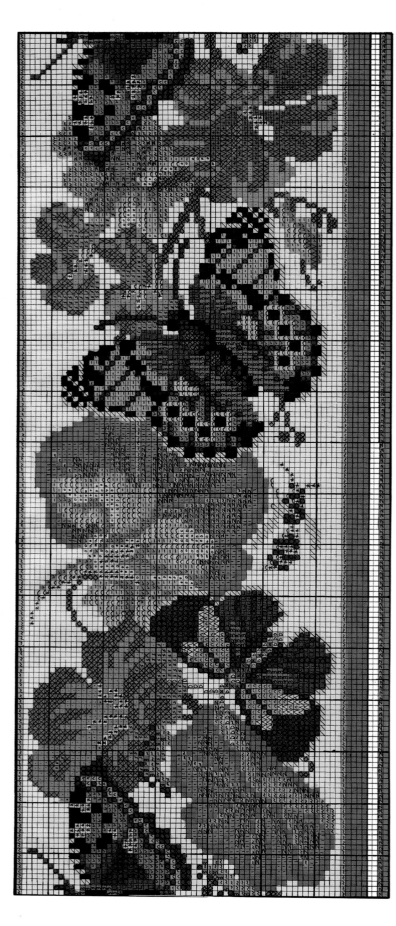

Wool colours and quantities

The quantities given below are the numbers of yards of Elizabeth Bradley Wool needed to work the various components of the Nasturtium Border and for joining and edging a six-panel carpet. The border and carpet squares are worked on 10 mesh interlock canvas using cross stitch.

Colours used:
30 including 1 background colour.

The background colour of all the Nasturtium Border pieces and the six central squares is pale green (J2).

Number on Chart key	Elizabeth Bradley Wool colour	Quantity (yards)	
		A corner	A sidepiece
1	A6	5	8
2	A8	4	4
3	B7	5	–
4	B8	7	–
5	B9	9	6
6	B10	15	12
7	B11	10	12
8	C3	6	4
9	C4	9	9
10	C5	8	9
11	C6	2	–
12	C7	8	10
13	C11	5	–
14	D4	12	6
15	E1	8	6
16	E7	4	6
17	E11	9	8
18	G4	4	–
19	G8	17	19
20	G10	17	10
21	H2	–	2
22	H4	3	2
23	I4	29	15
24	I9	7	6
25	J2	84	57
26	J6	26	12
27	J7	24	10
28	J8	41	27
29	L3	3	6
30	N1	3	3

Note: The quantity of background wool used in this design is included in the above quantity for Key number 25, pale green (J2).

Wool colours and quantities – joining and edging a six-panel carpet.

Number on Chart key	Elizabeth Bradley Wool colour	Quantity (yards)
11	C6	160
23	I4	84
26	J6	130
28	J8	440

INSTRUCTIONS

Please read these instructions very carefully before starting your carpet.

- All the central squares of a carpet must measure 160 stitches by 160 stitches.

- Cross stitch is the most suitable stitch to use throughout. It produces thick square pieces of needlework with no distortion in shape. For a perfect result all the stitches in a carpet should be made in the same direction. This requires some forward planning which is discussed later in these instructions.

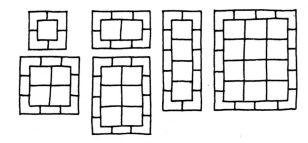

DIAGRAM 1: *To make a carpet with the Nasturtium and Butterfly Border, four corner pieces are always necessary. The number of pairs of side sections required depends on the size of carpet being made.*

Joining the Central Section of the Carpet

Each square in the central section of the carpet is separated from the next by a band of eight rows of stitches. The first two rows, one yellow ochre (C6) and the other grass green (J6) must be worked around each square separately before joining. The four rows of oak-leaf green (J8) between them join the squares together and are worked by overlapping the edges of the canvases and then stitching through them both.

Before working the first two rows of stitches (yellow ochre and grass green), CHECK CARE-FULLY that the square measures exactly 160 stitches by 160 stitches. If it does not, the carpet will not join up properly. If the finished pieces need stretching or blocking, do so before joining them together.

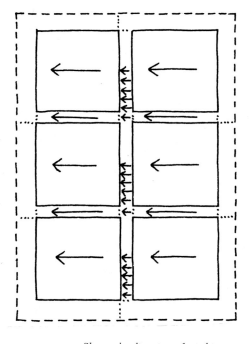

DIAGRAM 2 *Shows the direction of stitching.*

Once you have stitched the first two rows, decide on the arrangement of the edged squares of your carpet. They will be joined by four rows of stitches worked in oak-leaf green wool (J8). In the arrangement on page 101, the squares were joined in the following order: The Lily to The Iris, then The Pansy to The Auricula and lastly The Christmas Rose to The Cyclamen. Each pair of squares was then joined to the one below it.

To join together two pieces:

- Overlap the unworked canvas of the two pieces being joined, leaving a gap of four threads between the edges of the woolworks.

- Tack the layers of canvas in place carefully before stitching the joining rows of cross stitch. A "T"-shaped tack works best.

- Leave the underneath piece of canvas untrimmed.

- Trim the canvas of the top piece back to the fourth thread, cutting as near as possible to the fifth thread so that little ends of cut canvas are left sticking out – these will help to prevent thread four from unravelling. Snip off these little ends as you come to them when stitching.

- Where four squares join, the stitching will be through four pieces of canvas. Tack this section in place very carefully and be very gentle with the canvas at this point. If the canvas should unravel it will be more difficult to achieve a perfect join.

- The canvas sticking out at the back after joining can be trimmed up to the stitching line leaving a practically invisible join back and front.

- It takes practice to make a perfect join. The work will probably seem awkward and difficult to handle at first. With perseverance, though, this joining technique becomes easier and it is a very useful technique for joining two or more pieces of canvas together.

Attaching the Border

The border is made up of four corner sections and a variable number of side sections. For this carpet, six side sections will be needed, and each section is joined to the next with four rows of stitching.

To make the join, leave the last two rows at the ends of each border section unworked. Overlap the canvas and tack it in place as described on page 98 and then stitch the four missing rows of the border pattern through the double layer of canvas.

The border sections can be made separately and then joined together at the end when they are all complete, or they can be joined as the work progresses in a continuous and complete border. When stitching the border pieces (both corners and side sections), stitch only the pale green (I4) row of stitches on the inside edge. The border is then attached to the joined central squares using exactly the same method with the four green (J8) rows.

On the outside of the border sections, stitch the pale green (I4) row and the four green (J8) rows only. Leave the yellow ochre (C6) and the grass green (J6) rows until later when the carpet has been joined together.

Be very careful to work all the border sections correctly or they will not fit around the joined central squares. Count and check constantly as the work progresses.

All the stitches in the border should be made in the same direction to match the direction of the stitches on the central squares. So, the border must be planned according to the layout of the carpet. If the pieces of canvas have a selvedge this should be positioned on the right hand side and the pieces – as usual – should be stitched from right to left (see Materials and Methods).

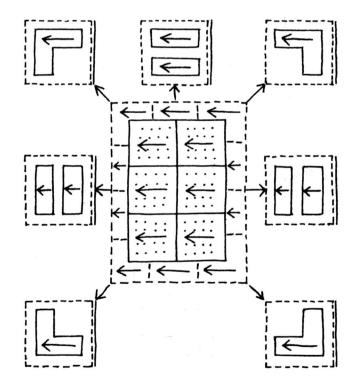

DIAGRAM 3: *The arrows show the direction of stitching on the various sections that make up a six-square carpet.*

Making a Neat Outside Edge for the Carpet

To finish off the carpet neatly:

- Trim any excess canvas at the joints; right up to the stitching line if desired.

- Trim the canvas all round the carpet to eight rows.

- Fold the canvas over at the edge and work the grass green (J6) row of stitches through both layers of the folded canvas. Leave two threads of the canvas unworked on the fold.

- Mitre the corners. To do this, make a fold diagonally across the canvas, three threads out from the edge of the stitching. Fold the edges of the canvas over and work the grass green (J6) row through four thicknesses of canvas where necessary.

- To make a neat bound edge, sew over the two remaining threads with the yellow ochre (C6) wool. First stitch one way, over and over all the way around the carpet and then stitch back the other way.

Finishing off the Back of the Carpet

If the carpet is to be laid on to a stone or wooden floor, then it should either be lined, or tacked to an insulating pad of carpet felt placed between the carpet and the floor.

Upholstery hessian makes a good traditional lining. To stop it from bagging, attach the hessian lightly to the back of the carpet with rows of tacking stitches.

If the carpet is to be laid on to a fitted carpet it is best left unlined as it will slip around less. Just hem or herringbone stitch hessian webbing or cotton tape over the raw edge of the folded canvas around the outside edge. The same tape can also be sewn over all the joints for added protection if required.

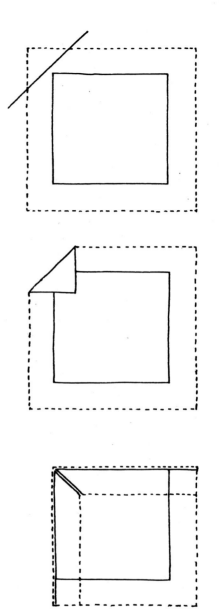

DIAGRAM 4: *Mitring the corners of a carpet.*

The carpet opposite has been made with six central squares. The Pansy, The Lily and The Cyclamen can be worked from the charts in this book or as kits. The Auricula is available as a kit only and The Christmas Rose and The Iris can only be worked from the charts in this book.

AUTUMN

A Wreath
of
Oakleaves

It is not growing like a tree
In bulk, doth make Man
better be;
Or standing long an oak, three
hundred year,
To fall a log at last, dry, bald,
and sere:
A lily of a day
Is fairer far in May,
Although it fall and die that
night –
It was the plant and flower
of Light.
In small proportions we just
beauties see;
And in short measure life
may perfect be.

"The Noble Nature", Ben Jonson
(1573-1637)

The oak is the largest and longest-lived British tree. It is often used to symbolize Britain, and pictures showing its typical sturdy trunk and spreading branches crowned with a great mop of leaves do seem to indicate that an item is British without need of further explanation. Oak leaves and acorns are used as the emblem of the National Trust, an organization devoted to the restoration and maintenance of some of Britain's finest houses and national monuments. The logo was particularly well chosen as oak leaves symbolize bravery, humanity and welcome.

British people worshipped the oak tree believing it to be the first tree ever created. It was sacred to a whole array of supreme gods including Zeus, Thor and Jupiter, or Jove. Oak trees were used as oracles and the future could apparently be divined by listening to the rustling of their leaves. The Druids venerated the oak tree and the sacred mistletoe that often grows upon it.

Anglesey, where I live, was the last Druid stronghold in Britain and the whole island was once covered in magnificent oak groves. Oak was essential for the building of sailing ships and from the sixteenth century onwards oak trees were felled so that the wood could be used in the ships of Britain's defensive fleet. Gradually, the island became almost totally deforested and even now, comparatively few oaks grow on the island.

Oak trees were once used to mark parish boundaries, and many splendid solitary oaks remain to remind us of the custom. They were very useful trees as apart from their obvious value as a source of wood for buildings, furniture and ships, their acorns were used as "pannage", or fattening fodder, for hogs. Their bark was necessary for the tanning of animal hides and a decoction made from it was an old remedy for diarrhoea and dysentery.

Needless to say there are superstitions and legends centred around such an ancient tree although they are surprisingly few considering the respect with which it has always been held. In country lore, there are many old rhymes and beliefs concerned with forecasting the weather and one associated with the oak tree goes as follows: "Oak before Ash, only a splash; Ash before Oak, in for a soak."

Myth is contradictory as to whether it is wise or unwise to stand under an oak tree in a thunder storm. One rhyme advises: "Strike Elm, strike Rowan, Not the Oak", whereas another counsels: "Beware of an Oak, It draws the Stroke." The verse continues: "Avoid the Ash, it courts the flash; Creep under the Thorn, it will save you from harm."

In art, a fallen oak symbolized the conversion of the pagan, and was the seal of the popes Sixtus IV and Julius II. The royal house of Stuart adopted the tree as its emblem after Charles II escaped from his enemies by hiding in an oak tree. As a sign of loyalty, small oak leaves and acorns were sometimes embroidered on to personal items such as pouches, garters and sashes.

The shape of an oak tree and the form of its leaves and fruit are particularly appealing and this, apart from historical and symbolic connotations, is enough to guarantee the oak a place on many pieces of antique needlework. Small sturdy oak trees adorn numerous stumpwork pictures and caskets while acorns and oak leaves are seen on samplers and on all sorts of canvaswork pieces throughout the sixteenth and seventeenth centuries. The Victorians stitched oak wreaths and sprigs on to many woolwork pieces, they were especially popular on items of men's clothing such as braces, waistcoats, slippers and smoking caps.

Oak leaves and acorns are the emblem of Scotland's Stuart Kings while woven woollen tartans are the distinctive fabric of the clans. Both are interwoven in the complicated strands of Scotland's long and sometimes bloody history. Shooting and fishing are still very much part of modern Scottish life and this tartan chair, with its cushion and a footstool embroidered with oak leaves on a tartan background, could be found in any Highland shooting lodge.

Wool colours and quantities

The quantities listed below are the numbers of yards of Elizabeth Bradley Wool needed to work a circular piece 114 stitches in diameter on 10 mesh interlock canvas using cross stitch.

Colours used:
23 including 7 background colours
(Key numbers 1-7, below).

Number on Chart key	Elizabeth Bradley Wool colour	Quantity (yards)
1	A5	22
2	A6	42
3	A7	24
4	C6	20
5	L10	10
6	M11	17
7	N10	19
8	E2	4
9	E3	4
10	E4	4
11	F10	4
12	F11	4
13	G5	4
14	G6	4
15	I2	10
16	I4	15
17	I6	13
18	I7	3
19	I9	10
20	I11	9
21	J6	5
22	J7	15
23	J8	15

Come, cheer up, my lads! 'tis to glory we steer,
To add something more to this wonderful year;
To honour we call you, not press you like slaves,
For who are so free as we sons of the waves.
Hearts of oak are our ships,
Hearts of oak are our men,
We always are ready,
Steady! Boys! Steady!
We'll fight and we'll conquer again and again.

"Heart of Oak", David Garrick (1717-79)

Wool colours for red tartan background

Number on Chart key	Elizabeth Bradley Wool colour
1	A5
2	A6
3	A7
4	C6
5	L10
6	M11
7	N10

Wool colours for blue tartan background

Number on Chart key	Elizabeth Bradley Wool colour
1	A6
2	C6
3	L2
4	L5
5	L7
6	M11
7	N1

Wool colours for purple tartan background

Number on Chart key	Elizabeth Bradley Woold colour
1	A5
2	A6
3	K10
4	L10
5	N1
6	N3
7	N8

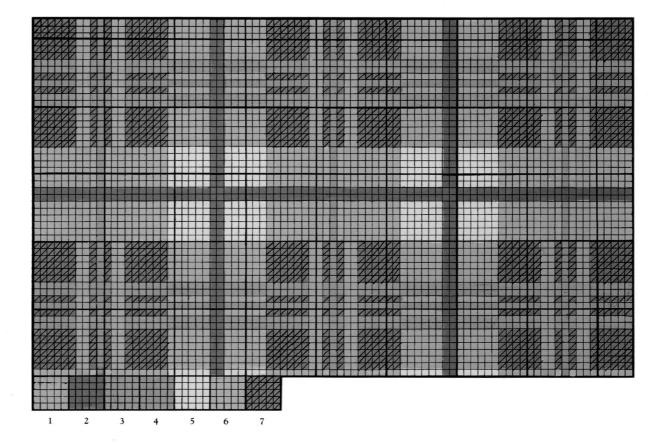

1   2   3   4   5   6   7

Tartan

The term plaid covers any arrangement of horizontal and vertical lines other than checks. These lines, though repeated regularly and in sequence, are not evenly spaced from one another and the colour of the rectangular or square blocks between them can vary as the pattern progresses. This type of pattern arose from the nature of the weaving process. The vertical lines are the warp threads which are set up on the loom, and the horizontal pattern is added gradually as the weft threads are added from the shuttle. Plaids can be printed or woven and many countries have their own distinctive colours and traditional patterns.

The word plaid comes from the Gaelic word for blanket and Scottish woven woollen plaids, known as tartan, are probably the best known in the world. Each clan has its own tartan and each tartan has two versions: dress and hunting.

Tartan patterns can be used to make very smart pieces of finished needlework. The charts are easy to follow and yet interesting to work. The tartan design shown here is not based on any particular clan tartan, it is merely a harmonious and reasonably interesting plaid in three colourways. Mellow colours were chosen rather than bright shades because they tend to be more useful in decorating schemes and are autumnal in feel. The same pattern worked in a mixture of pastel colours would also be appealing and could be smart in a baby's room or pale bedroom. Primary colour plaids could also be fun and would resemble some of the delicious Provençal plaids printed in France in the early nineteenth century.

AUTUMN

The Pansy

Amongst these roses in a row,
Next place I pinks in plenty,
These double daisies then
for show,
And will not that be dainty?
The pretty pansy, then I'll tye,
Like stones some chain encasing;
The next to them their near ally,
The purple violet placing.

"Muses Elysium", Michael Drayton
(1563-1631)

"God send thee hartes ease. For it is much better with poverty to have the same, then to be a kyng, with a myserable mynde"

Bulwarke of Defence, Bullein (1562)

Pansies flower so energetically and for so long that they literally exhaust themselves to the point of total extinction and have to be grown from seed every year in order to maintain a stock of good plants. Because they flower for such a long period they seem to have found their way into every chapter of this book. Britain's native pansy, the endearing heartsease or *Viola tricolor* is featured in the spring design, Primavera, while a big, bold, modern hybrid pansy is one of the flower circles in the summer section. The pansies featured in this design (on page 113) are called winter pansies because they flower through the winter, but they are also autumnal in that one actually buys and plants them in the autumn. Throughout the autumn, garden centres are full of their bright flowers. They tend to be simple flowers with single coloured, plain petals like the best silk velvet and with a small central eye rather than the elaborate faces and splashed and mottled petals of my favourite summer pansies. No summer garden is complete without some pansies but in winter they give a special pleasure.

"The wind is icy, and the snow patches are still here, but in the nearest garden I can get to I saw – one yellow pansy staring up at the sun astonished and reproachful because it had bits of frozen mud stuck to its little cheeks."

Elizabeth, Countess Russell (1899)

Like so many garden flowers pansies have their own stories and history. In legend, Cupid shot an arrow at a simple wild pansy. The wound caused the originally white flower to turn purple as is described by Oberon in William Shakespeare's *A Midsummer Night's Dream*:

That very time I saw, . . .
Flying between the cold moon and the earth,
Cupid all arm'd: a certain aim he took
At a fair vestal, throned by the west;
And loos'd his love-shaft smartly from his bow,
As it should pierce a hundred thousand hearts.
But I might see young Cupid's fiery shaft
Quench'd in the chaste beams of the
water'y moon,
And the imperial votaress passed on,
In maiden meditation, fancy-free.
Yet mark'd I where the bolt of Cupid fell.
It fell upon a little western flower –
Before milk white, now purple with
love's wound, –
And maidens call it love-in-idleness.

The petals of heartsease and other pansies, along with those of flowers such as nasturtium, marigolds and borage, can be used to decorate salads and jugs of Pimms. Compresses, ointments and infusions made from heartsease will help sufferers of asthma, convulsions, venereal disease and epilepsy. Not surprisingly, heartsease was also used to ease pains of the heart. A cordial made from the flowers was used to treat physical heart disease as well as the soreness of the heart due to the pangs of love.

Pansy Names

No flower has more names than the pansy. The historic *Viola tricolor* can be called love-in-idleness, three faces under a hood, heartsease, eyebright, cat's face, Jack-jump-up-and-kiss-me, bird's eye and many others. The name Johnny-jump-up is still used in America and the herbalist Nicholas Culpeper refers somewhat disapprovingly to yet another name, herb trinity. "Our physicians blasphemously call Phansies or Heartsease, a Herb of the Trinity, because it is of three colors." The plethora of names given to this small flower is an indication of the affection which it inspires. Talking about pansies in general, *The Florist's Museum* (published in 1837) tells us that: "The many

Pansies, Violas and Violettas

The Latin name of all garden hybrid pansies is the unwieldy *Viola wittrokiana*, whereas violas and violettas are grouped botanically under the name *Viola williamsii*. There seems to be a certain amount of confusion as to what is the difference between violas, pansies and violettas. All three belong to the large family Violaceae which contains more than 450 species, some of which grow wild in most countries in the world. Generally speaking, a viola or violetta flower is smaller and more compact than a pansy and does not show the whisker-like markings that give pansy faces their endearing expressions. Ruskin apparently devoted four pages of *The Garden of Prosperina* to trying to define the differences between pansies and violas without reaching any very clear conclusion.

The confusion between the species is largely caused by the interbreeding of various violas to develop bigger and better varieties. *Viola cornuta*, *Viola tricolor* and *Viola lutea* are three that played a large part in the story of the modern pansy. *Viola cornuta*, the horned violet, is a native of southern Europe. The flowers of this delightful and delicate viola are white or pale blue and seem to hover like a cloud of butterflies over a mass of heart-shaped, bright green leaves. Other modern violas and pansies were made by crossing *Viola cornuta* with the yellow pansy, *Viola lutea* called by Parkinson in 1626, "The great yellow Pansy, which better abideth our winters".

The Development of the Modern Pansy

The simple heartsease is one of the most ancient of garden plants, it has flowered unchanged for many centuries. Its development into a more elaborate florist's flower began comparatively late and to-

names which have been given to the generally humble but highly interesting flowers which compose the genus viola, are proofs of the high estimation in which they have been held in all ages."

The name pansy is derived from the French, Pensee, a thought. ". . . there is Pansies , that's for thoughts," says Ophelia in *Hamlet*. In the language of flowers, it is therefore not surprising to find that the pansy means "you occupy my thoughts", or remembrance.

OVERLEAF: *A Delpht rack hanging on a natural brick wall is filled with pansy plants in terracotta pots. They are interspersed with pictures and books which could be helpful in the painting of a pansy design such as the one shown below.*

Wool colours and quantities

The quantities listed below are the numbers of yards of Elizabeth Bradley Wool needed to work a piece measuring 160 stitches by 160 stitches on 10 mesh interlock canvas using cross stitch.

Colours used:
18 plus 1 background colour.

The background colour of the square shown on page 101 is pale green (J2). The background colour of the piece on page 109 is black (G11).

Number on Chart key	Elizabeth Bradley Wool colour	Quantity (yards)
1	A5	16
2	A6	17
3	A8	19
4	D5	5
5	I4	19
6	I6	28
7	J5	20
8	J7	27
9	J6	12
10	J8	25
11	M4	11
12	M5	25
13	M6	17
14	M10	20
15	M11	15
16	N11	17
17	N10	24
18	N9	25

Background quantity for a piece measuring 160 stitches by 160 stitches: 210 yards.

gether with another tardy entry, the dahlia, brought the number of florists flowers up to ten. The possibilities for the "improvement" of the pansy were seen by two gardeners at about the same time, each quite unaware of the other.

The first was Lady Monke who planted an array of little heartsease plants in a heart-shaped bed in her garden at Walton on Thames in the early years of the nineteenth century. The seed from the best of these plants was interbred with that of a fine, large-flowered, blue pansy newly brought from Holland and acquired by her gardener William Richardson. Between them they developed about 20 varieties that played a significant part in the development of the modern flower.

The second was Lord Gambier's gardener, Mr Thompson, who came to be known as "Father of the Heartsease" for his work of selection and hybridization. He used *Viola tricolor*, *Viola lutea* and *Viola altaica*, a native of the Crimea, in his experiments. By 1835, over 400 named cultivars were available and it was reported that "There is perhaps no instance in the annals of history of so rapid an increase among any one natural family of plants as in that of the pansy . . . such an increase furnishes a wonderful proof of the progress of floriculture throughout England."

The form of these new pansies changed greatly during their development. Shape became all-important; the main criteria for excellence being that the flowers should be, as near as possible, totally round. In order to display the attributes of their prized specimens, gardeners grew their plants in flower beds of all shapes and sizes and even William Robinson who was normally acerbic on the practice of bedding out wrote, "Pansies in great variety" were worthy of special treatment and should be grown "away from the confusion and weariness of the ordinary flower border."

Pansies were grown in urns and pots and all manner of elaborate containers, they were popular plants for filling the box-edged compartments of knot gardens and for putting in hanging baskets and wire plant stands. The most charming of all the extravagant Victorian concepts for growing pansies was a flowerbed modelled on a basket. In one example that I have seen locally, the sides of the basket are formed from a circle of simple, metal flowerbed edging with a semi-circular iron hoop over the top as a handle. Ivy has been grown over the handle and around the edges of the basket and then trimmed to make it neat. With different varieties of pansy flowering throughout most of the year, the basket need never be empty. I wish I had room to attempt something similarly attractive in my garden.

Many charming, watercolour studies of pansies were painted in the nineteenth century when the popularity of the large-flowered, fancy pansy was at its height. With their floral message of "you occupy my thoughts" they often appear on Valentine cards. Though not as popular as the rose with Victorian embroideresses, pansies can be seen on many pieces of Berlin woolwork. Their blotched and whiskered faces peer out engagingly from among the cabbage roses, forget-me-knots, lilies and poppies in the baskets and bunches of mixed flowers that were such great favourites with needlewomen of the day.

The Pansy Design

Three, fine, winter-flowering pansies were chosen as the models for this design. The pale, lavender blue, soft purple and mellow crimson of their petals are just three of the many colours available. They blend well together to make a charming trio of the large, friendly flowers.

1   2   3   4   5   6   7   8   9   10   11   12   13   14   15   16   17   18

AUTUMN

Autumn Patchwork

"... We learned to sew patchwork at school, while we were learning the alphabet; and almost every girl, large or small, had a bed-quilt of her own begun, with an eye to future house furnishing. I was not over fond of sewing, but I thought it best to begin mine early ... I liked assorting those little figured bits of cotton cloth, for they were scraps of gowns I had seen worn, and they reminded me of the persons who wore them."

A New England Girlhood,
Lucy Larcom, (1889)

Although strictly speaking this is a book about flowers and flower designs for working in woolwork, it would not be complete without including some small-scale repeating designs and geometric patterns. Patchwork is a craft in which innumerable little pieces of fabric are fashioned into shapes and then sewn together to make lengths of piecework, or patchwork. A design for patchwork needlework seemed a good way to feature many small, useful patterns that could be worked separately or would combine to be one grand interlocking design. Patterns such as these are invaluable for backgrounds and companion pieces to the bigger and more elaborate flower designs to be found in other sections of this book. Not all of the patches have flowery themes but the colours throughout are distinctly autumnal and many of the motifs suggest the countryside and garden.

Autumn-coloured Wools

Rich and mellow, autumn-coloured wools are a joy to work with. The opulent golds, yellows, russets, oranges and flames make it seem as though one is handling skeins of distilled sunshine rather than mere hanks of wool; such colours are reminiscent of the diffuse golden sunlight seen in the paintings of some Renaissance masters. These and other autumn colours contribute to a general impression of old paint and the patina of ages. There are the dark browns of wet astringent earth, the vermilion, scarlet and crimson of berries and fungi, the olive greens, ochres and cinnamon of fading leaves and the purples and mauves of Michaelmas daisies and blackberries. Living next to the sea, blue also becomes an autumn colour, the sea merges with the sky at the horizon and both are the same soft, greeny blue of sea warmed and gilded by autumn sunshine.

Patchwork Quilts

Patchwork and quilting are traditional women's crafts in both Britain and America. A quilt is a textile sandwich with a layer of fabric top and bottom and a filling of wool or cotton in the middle to give warmth. The top may be plain, patchwork or appliqué or a combination of the three. Quilting was introduced to Europe from the Orient and Near East in the early Mediaeval period. Quilted jerkins were used as rudimentary protection against spears and swords in battle and later quilted under garments were made to protect the skin from abrasive metal armour. By the eighteenth century quilting was widely used and had become decorative as well as simply a way to keep layers of fabric together. Intricate patterns were stitched on to breeches, petticoats and waistcoats as well as the pieces of quilted cloth used as bedcovers that became known simply as quilts.

My favourite British patchwork quilts are those made from hundreds of small fragments of "painted callicoes" or "chints" which were patterned fabrics that were imported from India in the seventeenth century. Scraps of this precious chintz were collected and when enough had been gathered together a quilt was made. The little pieces of fabric were fashioned into patches in the shape of hexagons, diamonds or squares before being joined together with tiny stitches. Often the expanse of neat, chintz patches was enlivened by a large panel in the middle showing a printed fabric basket or bouquet of flowers.

All the little pieces of fabric seem to combine together in these quilts to make a particularly rich and fascinating whole. Sometimes such a quilt can be a complete archive of fabric designs in itself and they are highly collectible both for the decorative qualities and the design value of their fabrics. They are objects of such obvious attraction that, independent of fashion, they have always been treasured, which is why, perhaps, so many examples have survived in excellent condition to the present day.

An area of pattern from the Autumn Patchwork carpet shown on page 122.

Greek key border

Wool colours and quantities of Elizabeth Bradley wool needed to work the border on the carpet shown on page 122 using cross stitch.

Number on Chart key	Elizabeth Bradley Wool colour	Quantity (yards)
1	C11	64
2	C6	194
3	G8	166

American Quilts

Pioneers carried pieced coverlets and quilts with them to their new homes in the New World as part of their household goods. Once established in their new home, the women of America took the basic art of quilt making one step further and transformed a traditional craft into what was to become a very special and interesting part of American history.

Apart from their obvious value as a warm bedcover, quilts were a part of a girl's upbringing. Like samplers, they were seen as evidence of a certain level of accomplishment. As a general rule, each young girl would work several patchwork-spreads or covers in her teens and then stow them away in her bridal chest in readiness for her adult life. When she got betrothed or engaged, one of these pieced tops was chosen to be quilted and then used as a coverlet for her marriage bed.

"The quilting was in those days considered as the most solemn and important recognition of a betrothal. When a wedding was forthcoming, then there was a solemn review of the stores of beauty and utility thus provided, and the patchwork-spread best worthy of such distinction was chosen for the quilting. Thereto, duly summoned, trooped all intimate friends of the bride, and the quilt being spread on a frame, and wadded with cotton, each vied with other in the delicacy of the quilting they could put upon it; for quilting was also a fine art, and had its delicacies and nice points, concerning which grave, elderly matrons discussed with judicious care."

The Minister's Wooing,
Harriet Beecher Stowe, (1859)

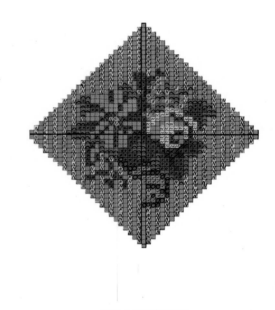

OPPOSITE: *This classic border is worked in three colours only and has a repeat of ten stitches. It is a very useful narrow border for making pieces of needlework appear more formal. It looks smart and decorative around the Autumn Patchwork carpet as seen on page 122. A worked sampler made into a small cushion can be seen in the photograph overleaf. Such small cushions can be useful when on trains and planes as travel pillows, filled with a suitable mixture of herbs they might help induce sleep as well as support the head. The alphabet in the centre is simple and basic to use and is often seen on late nineteenth-century samplers.*

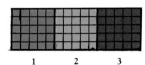

OVERLEAF: *Seeds, fruit and dried flowers have been arranged in shapes, boxes and compartments to reflect the diamond-shaped patches and geometric patterns of this design. The carpet and cushions have been worked from the charts on pages 120 and 121, and the border from the chart above.*

Chart 1: wool colours and quantities are overleaf

Chart 2: wool colours and quantities are overleaf

Wool colours and quantities

The quantities listed below are the numbers of yards of Elizabeth Bradley Wool needed to work a piece 299 stitches by 450 stitches (the area inside the border of the carpet shown to the right) on 10 mesh interlock canvas using cross stitch.

Colours used: 29 colours.

Number on Chart key	Elizabeth Bradley Wool colour	Quantity (yards)
1	A3	34
2	A5	161
3	A6	107
4	A7	73
5	A11	83
6	B4	136
7	B7	61
8	C3	57
9	C5	67
10	C6	71
11	C7	82
12	C11	104
13	D5	75
14	E1	197
15	E7	75
16	E10	39
17	G3	35
18	G8	60
19	G10	204
20	I7	63
21	I9	54
22	J6	186
23	J8	111
24	K6	160
25	K9	189
26	M11	86
27	N1	87
28	N2	75
29	N3	136

Wool quantities for the border worked around the Autumn Patchwork carpet are given on page 116.

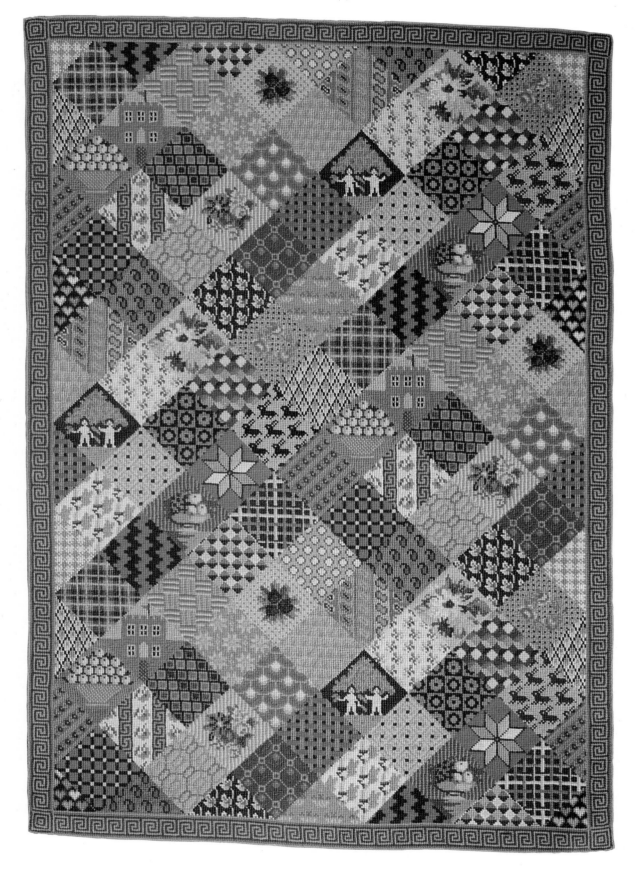

The Patchwork Design

From a distance, a length of woolwork stitched with this patchwork design would look very similar to a patchwork quilt from the middle of the last century. Many of the patterns resemble those found on the printed calicoes and cottons from that time. There are 38 different designs in all, spread over two charts each 150 stitches by 150 stitches. Some of the patterns are taken from old Berlin woolwork charts while others are little traditional sampler motifs repeated over and over again to make simple repeating patterns. The rest of the designs were made up as the chart progressed.

As far as possible, colours are mellow and autumnal and many of the little diamond-shaped patches feature autumnal motifs such as stars, chrysanthemums, late roses, and little brown leaves. Others show baskets of fruit, Adam and Eve under an apple tree, little rabbits, acorns and oak leaves. The little red sampler house is surrounded by red toadstools growing in the green grass. There are also two tartan patterns and many geometric ones. Each of the small patterns may be used separately as well as part of the patchwork design. Some of the simpler charts would be useful for stitching interesting and unusual backgrounds.

Wool colours can, of course, be changed to match individual colour schemes and tastes. Plain patches or patches worked with initials or simple stripes and checks can be interspersed among those on the charts to give a less elaborate overall appearance to the finished work.

Each of the two charts – 1 and 2 – measure 15ins by 15ins and are about the right size for making a cushion. If extended outwards they could be used to make excellent chair or stool seats. The two charts can also be organized to work together so that large pieces of patchwork suitable for rugs and carpets can be sewn. The manner in which these two basic charts are combined is of necessity quite complicated because so many different designs are involved. A plan to show how it is done is shown to the left.

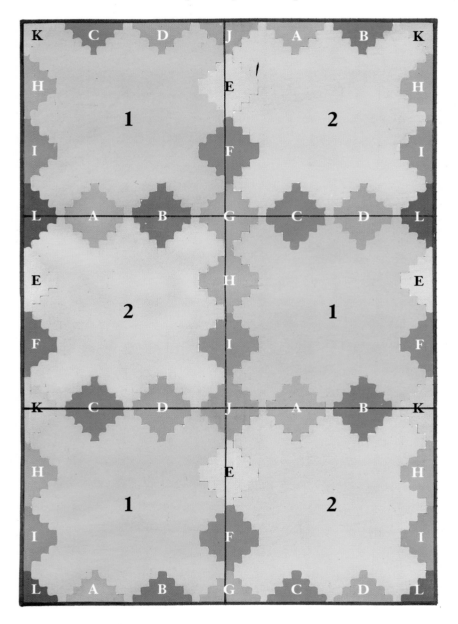

This plan shows how the two Autumn Patchwork charts 1 and 2 can be used together to make the carpet that is shown opposite.

WINTER

WINTER

Beauty's not always in a
scarlet robe.
She wears an old black shawl;
She flouts the flesh and shows
the bone
When winter trees are tall.
More beautiful than fact may be
The shadow on the wall . . .

Oh, fairer than young harlot
Summer proud
This subtle, crooked, wise
Old Winter croaks a
different truth
Scorning the sensuous lies;
Etches the finer skeleton
For more perceptive eyes.

"Winter", Vita Sackville-West
(1892-1962)

In the past, winter gardens were a picture of dripping dank shrubberies, empty flowerbeds and straggling rose trees. Recently, however, things have improved and it has now become fashionable to have a garden that is interesting and busy throughout all four seasons. Most gardening books devote at least a few chapters to telling us how to fill a garden with subtle colours, interesting shapes and some flowers all winter.

The season of winter brings its own special gardening pleasures and satisfactions and it should also be remembered that winter is a necessary evil if only so that we can better appreciate the joys of summer. Herbaceous plants and deciduous shrubs have flowered mightily in their season and need a rest, roses do not flourish without a winter break and many seeds will not sprout at all unless they get their dose of sub-zero temperatures. The gardener also deserves a fallow period and many look forward to winter as a quiet period for planning and reflection.

Whether winter is regarded with dread or anticipation there is no doubt that much of it is cold, wet and on the coast of Wales very windy. Winter gardening is certainly much more pleasant when the sun shines but whatever the weather there is always plenty to do and it is certainly not a season in which one can just sit back and admire the view from the window. A bit of effort now ensures a successful spring and autumn the following year and this is particularly true in a large garden when there are always lists of jobs to be finished.

Winter Tasks

One of the most pleasurable jobs in the garden at this time of year is pruning and cutting back. The form of trees and shrubs can be greatly improved by pruning and training and winter is a good time to tackle this task as the outline of the plants can be studied without all the summer greenery getting in the way. Shapes can be kept natural or be formalized by judicious clipping and training over frames or up walls.

Hedges and all sorts of topiary are at their loveliest in winter especially with a light covering of frost or snow to emphasize their shape. The textures and different greens of the various trees and shrubs form a tapestry landscape all of their own. Avenues and towers, domes, birds, balls and even a whole chess set or hunting scene complete with horses, fox and hounds have been cut in yew to stand silent and impressive against green winter lawns and cold grey, snow-laden skies.

Many gardeners leave seed heads and the dry stalks of herbaceous plants to stand in their flower beds, both for the sake of the birds and because they can look wonderful when outlined with rims of white frosty rime. Other gardeners like their flowerbeds to be tidy and cut them down close to the earth; they have to rely on berries and the bird table to bring winter birds to the garden.

Wintry Delights

Architectural plants such as phormium and yuccas give structure to the winter garden, they fully justify their place there at this time of year. The dogwoods are also good value, they do not flower conspicuously, but their crimson, vermilion or yellow stems gleam and glow on frosty mornings. Leafless twigs, lacy against the sky complement the imposing tasseled bulk of *Garrya elliptica*, and the untidy masses of mahonia are made worth while by their lemon yellow, scented flowers.

Each pleasure taken for granted in summer is intensified in winter, each new bud or shoot or insignificant flower really appreciated. Winter jasmine with its spiky stems and starry, yellow flowers seems to be in bloom all season. Clematis too, has

PREVIOUS PAGE: *These two woolwork stockings were made from the chart on page 140. They are being packed with the customary mixtures of toys and sweets. Small items made from needlework make good Christmas gifts and a selection of pieces made from the alphabet and border designs on pages 21 and 46 can be seen among the pine branches.*

its winter varieties which though less colourful than later hybrids seem particularly exquisite in the coldness and bareness of the winter garden. *Clematis armandii* is evergreen with green-white elegant blooms while *C. cirrhosa* has charming bell-like flowers.

Scented flowers are especially welcome and surprisingly common among winter-flowering varieties of plants. My favourite winter shrub, *Viburnum bodnantense*, has clusters of sweet-smelling pale pink blossoms on its bare branches. Another shrub or small tree well worth growing is witch hazel which sports little spidery tufts of aromatic yellow or apricot flowers along its twigs. Daphnes will perfume the air on still days and chimonanthus, or wintersweet, grown against a wall smells of "violets and jonquils".

Some crocuses and snowdrops smell sweet if you get down close enough to them. Aconites don't have any scent as far as I know but their cheerful yellow buttercup flowers are very welcome nevertheless. Cyclamens are another winter plant that need close viewing to really appreciate the details of their marbled leaves and fluttering flowers. Vita Sackville-West called them "little frightened cyclamen with leveret ears laid back".

Even in cold and wet winter gardens conditions can vary enormously from one spot to another and it is worth taking care to site plants where they will grow best. *Iris stylosa* blooms where it is sunny, arid and dry whereas Christmas roses like it wherever the soil is rich, damp and shaded. The spotted leaved pulmonaria, or lungwort, does not seem too fussy and nor does *Arum italicum* with its smart, dark green leaves veined with white.

If, having grown all these flowers, the craving for colour still persists or the weather becomes too bad to go outside and enjoy the garden, then bring the garden into the house. Plant bowls and pans of early-flowering bulbs to flower inside. Large and showy hyacinths can be made to flower for Christmas, while daffodils and scented narcissi make marvellous winter pot plants. Perhaps even more charming are groups of small bulbs set among moss like miniature gardens. Jonquils, crocuses, chionodoxa and grape hyacinths can all be grown successfully in this way.

Another form of winter gardening is in the mind. Evocative pictures of summer gardens are conjured up by gardening books. Seed catalogues can lead to an orgy of lists which have to be seriously pruned when the individually modestly-priced packets add up to an alarming total. Last year's garden notebooks and diaries can be studied by those organized enough to have kept them and resolutions made to keep one by those who didn't.

Embroidering flowers with wool on canvas is another very creative and satisfying form of winter gardening. It could be regarded as a very mild form of exercise, keeps gardeners awake during the long dark evenings and can produce lasting and useful objects that are also good to look at.

The Winter Sampler

Silk colours and quantities

The quantities listed below are the numbers of skeins of DMC six-stranded perle cotton needed to work a sampler 163 stitches by 163 stitches. Each length of cotton should be split in half and the sampler worked with three strands only.

The sampler shown opposite was worked on 100% linen scrim, 91cms wide, which has approximately 20 threads to the inch. Each stitch should be worked over two threads.

Number on Chart key	DMC thread number	Number of skeins
1	355	3
2	221	1
3	834	1
4	831	4
5	ecru	2
6	3021	2
7	648	2
8	647	2
9	581	1-2
10	731	3
11	3362	2-3
12	501	2
13	890	4-5
14	502	2

The classic, Queen Anne, red-brick house on this sampler has been set in a topiary garden. It looks very right and proper there as topiary was going through one of its periods of popularity at the same time as such houses were being built.

Mature dark green and golden yews are cut into domes, tiers and peacocks on either side of the house. The season is Christmas and there is a beribboned holly wreath on the front door. More holly with bright red berries is mixed with ivy leaves and the clear yellow stars of winter jasmine to form a border. In classic Christmas card style, it is snowing and children have made a snowman on the snow-covered lawn. Robins peck at food put out for them to eat in the snowy garden.

Topiary is the term used for the clipping of evergreen trees and shrubs into unnatural shapes. The living green structures can be simple hedges or arches or intricate mazes though the term is more often used to refer to the wierd and wonderful shapes that can be created with time and much loving care. A parterre is an example of simple topiary in which, although the clipping and shape of the small, slow-growing hedges is kept fairly basic, an elaborate pattern is created over an area of garden. My sampler garden has a circle of low-cut yew hedge in the middle of the snowy lawn with a boundary of box balls.

"There are divers Sorts of Parterres . . . Parterres of embroidery are so called because the Box wherewith they are planted, imitates embroidery upon the Ground . . . Their Bottom should be sanded, the better to distinguish the Foliage and Flourish'd-work of the embroidery . . . "

From *The Theory and Practice of Gardening*, translated from the French by John James of Greenwich (1712)

Topiary is an art for patient gardeners, shapes made from evergreen trees and shrubs are not made in a year or even ten, but can take decades to reach perfection. Many varieties of evergreens can be clipped, but the most traditional are holly, cypress, bay, juniper, myrtle, box and yew.

The appreciation of the art of topiary comes and goes over the centuries; it is approved of in some and scorned in others. The Romans were master gardeners and one of the earliest descriptions of a topiary garden is by Pliny the younger in first century Tuscany. His box trees were cut into "monsters, animals, letters and the names of the master and the artificer". The art flowered again in Elizabethan gardens when Francis Bacon wrote, "I, for my part, doe not like Images Cut out in Juniper or other Garden stuffe: They be for Children. Little low Hedges, Round like Welts, With some Pretty Pyramides, I like well:" *Essays*, (1598)

Topiary gardens can be grand in the French manner of the great parterres of Vaux de Vicomte or in the Renaissance style at Villa Lante in Italy. Alternatively, they can be fantastic as in the gardens of Hampton Court Palace in 1599 where trees were cut into "centaurs, servants with baskets, and figures of men and women, all wrought in topiary". Dutch gardens, where all is crowded and in miniature, have a particular intimate charm which was transported over the Atlantic and can still be seen in the gardens of colonial Williamsburg.

Eighteenth-century landscape gardeners such as William Kent, Capability Brown and Repton despised the contrivance of topiary and were vitriolic and destructive in their condemnation. The Victorians relegated their tree clipping to cottage gardens and it was left to the Arts and Crafts movement at the end of the nineteenth century to save the remnants of past skills. The rescue has been completed and brought up to date at gardens such as Sissinghurst and Hidcote.

The Winter Sampler is framed by an interesting selection of evergreen leaves, berries and rose hips gathered from the countryside surrounding my house on Anglesey.

1 2 3 4 5 6 7 8 9 10 11 12 13 14

Wool colours and quantities

The quantities listed below are the numbers of yards of Elizabeth Bradley Wool needed to work a piece measuring 169 stitches by 169 stitches on 10 mesh interlock canvas using cross stitch.

Colours used:
14 plus 1 background colour.

When working the woolwork on the right from the chart on the left, the yellow line was omitted and four extra rows of background colour were worked around the edges.

The background colour used in the piece shown on page 2 is black (G11).

Number on Chart key	Elizabeth Bradley Wool colour	Quantity (yards)
1	B10	49
2	B11	16
3	D5	27
4	D11	29
5	F2	54
6	G8	41
7	H6	10
8	H7	10
9	I4	19
10	I7	33
11	J8	35
12	K5	39
13	K6	92
14	K9	28

Background quantity for a piece measuring 169 stitches by 169 stitches: 160 yards.

Here interwoven branches form
a wall,
And from the living fence green
turrets rise;
There ships of myrtle sail in
seas of box;
A green encampment yonder
meets the eye;
And loaded citrons bearing shields
and spears.

Alexander Pope (1688-1744)

Topiary is once more highly fashionable, the more whimsical and fantastic the better as long as its style complements the environment in terms of age and architecture. Fashion has once more turned full circle and the sarcastic list of topiary subjects quoted in an essay by Alexander Pope would be music to the ears of contemporary gardeners who are always on the lookout for new and unusual ideas.

Adam and eve in yew; Adam a little shattered
. . . Eve and the serpent very flourishing.
The tower of Babel, not yet finished.
St George in box; his arm scarce long enough,
but will be in condition to stick the dragon by
next April.
A green dragon of the same, with a tail of
ground ivy . . .
Edward the Black Prince, in cypress.
A laurestine bear in blossom, with a juniper
hunter in berries . . .
Divers eminent modern poets in bays, somewhat
blighted . . .
A quickset hog, shot up into a porcupine, by its
being forgot one week in rainy weather.
A lavender pig, with sage growing in its belly.
Noah's ark in holly, standing on the mount; the
ribs a little damaged for want of water.

The Christmas Rose

A little girl came one day to worship the Christ child as He lay in the manger. Her eyes filled with tears when she realized that she had no present to give to the baby. Gabriel the Archangel appears to the child and comforts her:

"Tell me, my little one – Why do
you weep?
Is it because He's so fast asleep?
See! I will wake Him," and
Gabriel smiled,
As he kissed the face of the
heavenly Child.

The little girl explains why she
is crying.

Then Gabriel answered, "Come,
child, with me,
The flowers you wish'd for you
soon shall see;"
And he led her forth to a place
most fair,
Where sweet blossoms scented
the sunlit air.

She smil'd to the angel in
glad delight,
And filled her hands with the
blossoms white;
Then ran with her burden of
roses sweet,
And laid them all down at the
Christ-child's feet.

"The Legend of the Christmas Rose",
The Glory of the Garden,
MG Kennedy-Bell, FRHS (1923)

The Christmas rose is the flower of the Nativity and of St Agnes who is the patron saint of young virgins. The generic name, Hellebore, is derived from two Greek words, *Hellion*, to kill and *bora*, food. The true Christmas rose is *Helleborus niger*, so-called because of its "heart or root, is black, while its face shines with a blazing white innocence . . .". Reginald Farrer described hellebores as ". . . one of the candours of the world, in all its forms, of a white and unchangeable flawlessness."

"This plant hath thicke and fat leaves of a
deep green colour, the upper part whereof
is somewhat bluntly nicked or toothed,
having sundry divisions or cuts, in some
leaves many, in others fewer. It beareth
Rose-fashioned floures upon slender
stems, growing immediatly out of the
ground an hand-full high, sometimes very
white, and oftentimes mixed with a little
shew of purple: which being vaded, there
succeed small husks full of blacke seeds:
the roots are many, with long blacke
strings comming from one head."

Of blacke Hellebore, Gerard's *Herbal* (1597)

Hellebore is associated with the treatment of madness and nervous disorders. The powdered roots were found to be efficacious in the treatment of King Proteus of Argos's daughters who were totally convinced that they had been changed into cows. Gerard tells us that, "A purgation of Hellebore is good for mad and furious men, for melancholy, dull and heavie persons, and briefly for all those that are troubled with blacke choler . . . " All in all, it would seem to be a thoroughly useful substance to have in one's medicine cupboard for alleviating moments of gloom and the moods of disgruntled spouses.

Four kinds of Hellebore are generally grown and all of them are well worth their place in any garden. *Helleborus niger* is the pure white Christmas rose. The variety "Potters Wheel" is one of the best and will produce magnificent flowers 3-4 ins (7.5-10 cms) across if the plant is well fed with manure. Another favourite is *Helleborus orientalis*, the Lenten rose, whose flowers can be ivory, greenish white or tinged with delicate pink and whose petals are often speckled with purple spots. For good value all year round, *Helleborus argutifolius* must be the winner. It is often in full flower by mid-winter and the generous bunches of greenish, cup-shaped flowers are held on stout stems 2 ft (60 cms) high.

Last, but not least, is *Helleborus foetidus*, the stinking hellebore and Britain's native species. This unappealing name is deceptive as this is a most attractive and very useful plant. It will grow almost anywhere and though the flowers are smaller then those of *H. argutifolius* they are delicate and of a bright and fresh pale green.

Hellebores seem to be rather fashionable at the moment and a lot of excellent, improved cultivars are coming on to the market. Selection and development is done by choosing the best out of batches of seedlings and is a slow process. In spite of this, the various species are coming on in leaps and bounds and I would not be at all surprised to see the Hellebore join the august ranks of florists' flowers before too long. It will make a charming new recruit.

The Christmas rose in this design is basically *Helleborus niger*, but I must admit to a few *H. orientalis*-like, purple spots and some rather unorthodox pink and green tingeing of the petals. These "improvements" were necessary to give structure and form to this pure but fairly featureless flower. The plant is growing from a mound of rich compost on which a very early snail is investigating the possibilities of a mid-hibernation snack.

This crisp, white winter table set for a simple dinner has been embellished with a large placemat made from the Christmas Rose design on page 134. The flowers have been worked against a soft, sea blue background (K8).

1 2 3 4 5 6 7 8 9 10 11 12 13 14 15 16 17 18 19 20 21 22 23 24 25 26 27

Wool colours and quantities

The quantities listed below are the numbers of yards of Elizabeth Bradley Wool needed to work a piece 160 stitches by 160 stitches on 10 mesh interlock canvas using cross stitch.

Colours used:
27 colours plus 1 background colour.

The background colour of the piece shown to the right is red (B11). The background colour of the piece shown on page 133 is blue (K8) and the colour of the Christmas rose used in the carpet shown on page 101 is pale green (J2).

Number on Chart key	Elizabeth Bradley Wool colour	Quantity (yards)
1	A9	13
2	A11	14
3	B2	17
4	D2	9
5	D4	6
6	F2	14
7	F3	27
8	F4	21
9	F5	14
10	F9	5
11	F11	30
12	G1	17
13	G4	9
14	G5	9
15	G9	42
16	H2	5
17	H3	5
18	H6	13
19	I1	10
20	I2	9
21	I4	24
22	I7	27
23	I8	5
24	J6	32
25	J8	30
26	J9	30
27	K7	19

Background quantity for a piece measuring 160 stitches by 160 stitches: 150 yards.

The lawn is like a lump of lead,
Your garden has been put to bed
And you have locked the potting-shed.

The snow has just commenced to fall,
The world is wrapped in winter's pall.
There are no signs of life at all.

When, like a star which shines at night,
That miracle of green and white –
A Christmas Rose creeps into sight:

A lonely herald of the Spring,
Of happy birds that nest and sing,
Of butterflies upon the wing,
Of fairies dancing in a ring –
And all that sort of thing.

"Christmas Roses", *Green Fingers* Reginald Arkell

WINTER

Evergreens and Christmas Festivities

The holly and the ivy,
When they are both full grown,
Of all the trees that are in the wood
The holly bears the crown.

The holly bears a blossom
White as the lily flow'r,
And Mary bore sweet Jesus Christ
To be our sweet saviour.

The holly bears a berry,
As red as any blood,
And Mary bore sweet Jesus Christ
To do poor sinners good.

The holly bears a prickle
As sharp as any thorn,
And Mary bore sweet Jesus Christ
On Christmas day in the morn.

The holly bears a bark
As bitter as any gall,
And Mary bore sweet Jesus Christ
For to redeem us all.

Anon.

Christmas makes the season of winter very special, for it adds glamour to what could be merely a cold and depressing time of year. The two are so interrelated that the scenes of frosty landscapes and snowy gardens so often seen on Christmas cards are what the word "winter" instantly conjures up in many people's minds. More realistic cards would show views with gales, wind, sleet, grey skies and rain.

Evergreens such as holly, ivy and mistletoe, with a supporting cast of Christmas trees and robins, are very much part of the idealized image of this season. The association of certain evergreens with the birth of Christ and the Nativity are so ancient that their origins are almost forgotten, yet they are so well established that even just a small picture of a sprig of spikey holly covered in brilliant red berries immediately brings Christmas to mind.

. . . But give me holly, bold and jolly,
Honest, prickly, shining holly;
Pluck me holly leaf and berry
For the day when I make merry.

"Give me Holly", Christina Rossetti (1830-94)

In the days when Christianity was very new in Britain, Pope Gregory suggested to St Augustine that he should try and adapt local pagan customs and festivals to merge with existing Christian feasts and beliefs. The Roman festival of Saturnalia occurred in the middle of winter on the 17, 18 and 19 December and some of its more acceptable rites were tacked on to the Christian Christmas celebrations. Every year at Saturnalia the Romans decorated their houses with holly and ivy and would exchange sprigs of holly to bring good fortune. Both holly and ivy were also part of the fertility rites of the Fire festival held on 25 December. The prickly holly symbolized the male, and the entwining ivy, the female participants of the rituals.

The early Christians were able to make a convincing case for the conversion of holly into the symbol for Christ's crown of thorns because of its prickly leaves. Ivy was rather more difficult to place as its leaves were not only part of fertility rites but they were also heavily associated with Bacchus, the Roman God of wine. Eventually, ivy came to symbolize the highly worthy virtues of friendship, fidelity and marriage and it was quietly allowed to join the other evergreens such as fir, bay and laurel without being given any special Christmas role.

The holly bears a berry red,
The ivy bears a black'un,
To show that Christ His blood did shed,
To save our souls from Satan.

Old English rhyme, Anon.

Mistletoe was even more troublesome to convert into a respectable evergreen as it was one of the most outrageously pagan of all plants. In one ancient Celtic ceremony the druids cut mistletoe boughs from sacred oak trees with golden sickles and caught them as they fell in pure white cloths held by four virgins. Then followed the sacrifice of white bulls and the distribution of the mistletoe to be hung above every doorway as a fertility symbol and a protection against witchcraft. Remnants of the past remain, and even today mistletoe is never hung in churches. Bunches of mistletoe are still hung over doorways at Christmas and the kissing that is obligatory under them could perhaps be seen as a first step towards fertility.

Today, holly is still thought to bring good fortune and to convey good wishes. Superstition says, however, that it should always be hung up before the mistletoe or ill luck will come down the chimney on Christmas Eve. Both evergreens must be removed by Epiphany on 6 January.

Christmas Eve, and all is ready for Father Christmas. Thomas is asleep, the empty stocking has been hung up and a glass of port and a mince pie are on the bedside table in case Father Christmas feels in need of refreshment.

He was dressed all in fur from his
head to his foot,
And his clothes were all tarnished
with ashes and soot;
A bundle of toys he had flung on
his back,
And he looked like a pedlar just
opening his pack.
His eyes how they twinkled! his
dimples how merry!
His cheeks were like roses, his
nose like a cherry;
His droll little mouth was drawn
up in a bow,
And the beard on his chin was as
white as the snow.
The stump of a pipe he held tight
in his teeth,
And the smoke it encircled his
head like a wreath.
He had a broad face, and a little
round belly
That shook, when he laughed,
like a bowl full of jelly.
He was chubby and plump – a
right jolly old elf –
And I laughed when I saw him,
in spite of myself . . .

A description of Father Christmas
from a "A visit from St Nicholas",
Clement Clark Moore (1822)

Christmas Past and Present

Christmas as we know it today is a comparatively recent invention. The elaborate decorations, the stylized Christmas meal of turkey and plum pudding, the wrapped parcels, cards, stockings and Christmas tree are all largely Victorian embellishments. The older Mediaeval and Tudor celebrations stretched over all 12 days between the Nativity and the Epiphany. Customs included the burning of the yule log, the crowning of the Lord of Misrule and long sessions of feasting, dancing and drunkenness.

Christmas was actually abolished by Oliver Cromwell in the seventeenth century and though it was restored after a few years of general gloom and complaints it did not really recover its former robust ebulliance until Victoria came to the throne. She and her husband, Albert, really enjoyed Christmas and gradually helped to change it into the intimate family and children's festival that it is today. Sentiment and the need for benevolence were added to this new romantic picture of Christmas by Charles Dickens in A Christmas Carol. Poor, half starved and crippled Tiny Tim, deprived of a proper Christmas wrung the hearts of the nation.

The miserable living conditions caused by the industrial revolution and mass movement of the population to the towns gave the memory of rural life and country Christmasses a distinctly rosy glow. A wave of nostalgia for the "good old days" swept through Victorian Britain and remnants of the hankering for this idealized Christmas past can still be seen on Christmas cards. All those coaches and horses and rubicund squires show an extremely romanticized picture.

"Time was when the frost was on the pane, and snow lay thick upon the ground, when all the chimneys smoked and all the ovens were full . . . When all were full of gladness and both serf and squire, baron and retainer, did their very best to keep their companions happy. All classes gave themselves up to frolic and revelry, with a thoroughness of spirit."

Christmas in the Olden Times, 1859 from
A Celebration of Christmas Caroline Harrington

It sometimes seems in the late twentieth century that so many customs and delights are crowded into the few days of Christmas that the whole reason behind it is almost forgotten. A great reminder of what it is all about is provided in the words of those traditional Christmas songs, the Christmas carols.

In the bleak midwinter,
Frosty wind made moan,
Earth stood hard as iron,
Water like a stone;
Snow had fallen, snow on snow, snow on snow,
In the bleak midwinter long ago . . .

Our God, heaven cannot hold him
Nor earth sustain;
Heaven and earth shall flee away,
When he comes to reign.
In the bleak midwinter a stable-place sufficed
The Lord God almighty, Jesus Christ.

Christina Rossetti (1830-94)

WINTER

A Christmas Stocking

The tradition of hanging up stockings for Father Christmas to fill with small gifts is another Victorian adaptation of an earlier custom. The bearded and jovial Father Christmas, described in CC Moore's poem, was based on Saint Nicholas who was a rich and extremely generous bishop living in Asia minor in the fourth century. He was much given to distributing alms and presents to the poor and the story goes that one Christmas morning a cottager found a bag of gold in a stocking hung up to dry before the fire. Saint Nicholas had apparently tossed it casually down the chimney as he passed by. Children have hung up stockings at the end of their beds ever since and parents acting for Saint Nicholas have filled them.

After the Reformation in Britain, saints became *persona non grata* and the character of the saintly

bishop was combined with the image of the jolly drunken spirit of mediaeval Christmas called Old Christmas or Sir Christmas who appears in miracle plays, masques and early carols. The result was Father Christmas, who is good and kind but also very jolly.

Embroidered Christmas Stocking

Christmas stockings tend to be large, long and hand knitted, the theory being that the bigger the stocking the more will be put in it. Special stockings made out of woolwork have become very popular, they make charming and manageable needlework projects and can be brought out every year like favourite tree decorations.

Most embroidered stockings are decorated all over with typical seasonal motifs and pictures. For a change, the one shown on the charts on page 140 is designed to actually look like a large sock with a realistically worked heel and toe. The foot and leg of the stocking are covered in a cheerful Victorian repeating pattern worked in bright colours and the ribbed area at the top features a row of small Christmas trees growing in cherry red pots.

Potting up fir trees and bringing them into the house is another Christmas custom popularized by Queen Victoria and Prince Albert. The trees were hung with small presents and decorations made out of tin and coloured glass. Real candles were attached to the branches and these were lit on Christmas Eve. A Christmas tree covered with lighted candles is a magical sight but unfortunately a very dangerous and inflammable one so that now tiny twinkling electric lights tend to be used instead of candles.

Making a Christmas Stocking

You will need to work the two sides of the stocking with the foot of one side facing to the left and the foot of the other side to the right. The pattern of the two sides will not match up exactly along the sides when they are joined. The joining can either be done by hand or with a sewing machine.

Wool colours and quantities

The quantities listed below are the numbers of yards of Elizabeth Bradley Wool needed to work one side of a stocking measuring 20ins long on 10 mesh interlock canvas using cross stitch.

Colours used: 15 colours

Number on Chart key	Elizabeth Bradley Wool colour	Quantity (yards)
1	A4	39
2	B9	6
3	B10	8
4	B11	39
5	C2	7
6	C3	8
7	C5	19
8	C6	59
9	J6	50
10	J11	6
11	J8	10
12	M10	39
13	N9	7
14	N10	8
15	N11	3

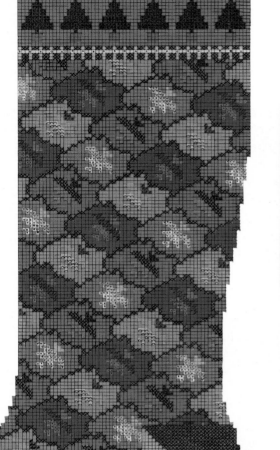

Please note that the symbols on the right foot chart are back to front.

WINTER
A Christmas Pudding

The only excuse for including a Christmas pudding in a book about flowers is the sprig of holly which custom dictates should be placed on top and which is put there to bring good fortune to those who eat the pudding. I have wanted to paint a plum pudding design for some years and this section of the book seemed a good place to slip one in.

Christmas puddings, or plum or figgy puddings, are a Victorian version of traditional plum porridge. This rich and highly indigestible dish was made by boiling beef and veal with sack, sherry and lemon and orange juice. The resulting stock was laced with alcohol, thickened with breadcrumbs, spiced with cinnamon, nutmeg and ginger and sweetened with brown sugar, dried fruit and prunes. By the beginning of the nineteenth century, suet had been substituted for the meat

stock and the porridge had become solid enough to be called a pudding. It is usually served with brandy butter and white sauce or custard.

Traditionally, Christmas puddings and cakes should all be made by the last Sunday before Advent which is sometimes known as Stir-Up Sunday. Each member of the family should stir the pudding mixture in turn and make a wish at the same time. After the stirring, small "silver" coins wrapped in little squares of greaseproof paper should be added for luck. Some pudding makers pop in a coin to bring good fortune, a ring for marriage and a thimble for a blessed life.

Rich, dark figgy puddings make a fitting finale to Christmas dinner. They used to be round like the one in this design because instead of being steamed in a basin like modern puddings they were wrapped in a muslin cloth and then suspended in a washing copper to cook. Christmas puddings should be served alight with blue brandy flames. To get the brandy to ignite is easier written about than done. The secret is to warm it well before pouring it over the pudding and setting it alight.

> "I always spell plumb-pudding with a b, p-l-u-m-b, I think it reads fatter and more suetty."
>
> Charles Lamb (1807)

The Christmas Pudding Design

This small square chart is a perfect design for making small Christmas presents. Woolwork kettle holders backed with felt were traditional Victorian gifts and the principle could be extended to making long double oven gloves or small square oven cloths with a loop on one corner to hang them up with.

Well-stuffed Christmas pudding pincushions would make cheerful and unusual Christmas presents. If after eating Christmas dinner you can still face the thought of Christmas pudding, then making a woolwork version might be a good project for the days between Christmas and New Year.

Wool colours and quantities

The quantities listed below are the numbers of yards of Elizabeth Bradley Wool needed to work a piece 64 stitches by 63 stitches on 10 mesh interlock canvas using cross stitch.

Colours used: 17 colours.

Number on Chart key	Elizabeth Bradley Wool colour	Quantity (yards)
1	A6	4
2	A7	3
3	B3	10
4	B4	10
5	B11	6
6	C1	5
7	C2	5
8	E7	4
9	E10	5
10	E11	5
11	G8	7
12	F3	3
13	F5	5
14	F10	8
15	G9	8
16	G10	7
17	K7	10

"In half a minute Mrs Cratchit entered – flushed, but smiling proudly, with the pudding, like a speckled cannon-ball, so hard and firm, blazing in half of half-a-quartern of ignited brandy, and bedight with Christmas holly stuck into the top. Oh, a wonderful pudding!"

A Christmas Carol,
Charles Dickens (1812-70)

Victorian kettle holders were often made from small squares of woolwork backed with felt. A modern kettle holder and a pin cushion both made from the design above can be seen above a Christmas pudding sprigged with holly.

WINTER

The Robin

The robin is the Christmas bird and the gardener's friend; Donne calls it the "household bird with the red stomacher". They are tame, companionable birds, happy to perch near to a gardener and wait for grubs and worms to be unearthed for them to eat. In Britain, to kill a Robin was regarded as a sacrilege but in Europe robins were regarded as tasty morsels – one French recipe describes how a large chicken can be stuffed with foie gras, truffles and robins. It is not really surprising that French robins are shy and nervous birds.

Robins stay with us all year round, their red breasts making them stand out clearly against the snow in the winter garden. Both male and female robins have the same distinctive plumage and are difficult to tell apart. Juveniles are spotted and streaked olive-brown and buff and have a mottled breast rather than the usual red. A number of legends describe how the robin got his red breast. The most widely quoted story tells how the little bird tried to help Christ on the road to Calvary by attempting to remove the crown of thorns from His head. In his efforts, the robin's breast became bloodstained and ever afterwards robins have had red breasts. Another less known Mediaeval legend describes how the robin tried to assuage the thirst of souls in hell by taking drops of water to them in his bill. His breast became red and scorched as he flew to and fro through the flames.

The jolly little robin is, in fact, rather a thug and both sexes spend much of their time either evicting other robins from their territory or threatening to do so. In the heat of battle, one robin will sometimes go so far as to actually kill another. Recently, my mother found two such protagonists side by side on the lawn, they had killed each other in a fierce fight to the death. Male and female robins also fight and are only civil to each other in the breeding season.

Therefore all seasons shall be sweet to thee,
Whether the summer clothe the general earth
With greenness, or the redbreast sit and sing
Betwixt the tufts of snow on the bare branch
Of mossy apple-tree, while the nigh thatch
Smokes in the sun-thaw; whether the
eave-drops fall
Heard only in the trances of the blast,
Or if the secret ministry of frost
Shall hang them up in silent icicles,
Quietly shining to the quiet Moon.

Part of a poem to a sleeping child,
Samuel Taylor Coleridge (1772-1834)

This woolwork robin set against falling snowflakes and a deep grey, mid-winter sky has made a charming centrepiece to an octagonal picture frame and a twiggy beribboned wreath. They help to create a decorative and festive Christmas mantelpiece.

Wool colours and quantities

The quantities listed below are the numbers of yards of Elizabeth Bradley Wool needed to work a piece measuring 81 stitches by 81 stitches on 10 mesh interlock canvas using cross stitch.

Colours used:
16 colours including 1 background colour.

The background colour of the piece surrounded by a twig wreath on page 145 is ochre (C6). The sky colours of both the pieces shown are dark grey (H10) and cream (F3).

Number on Chart key	Elizabeth Bradley Wool colour	Quantity (yards)
1	B10	8
2	B11	4
3	C6	52
4	F3	9
5	H1	4
6	F8	5
7	F10	8
8	F11	8
9	G10	3
10	F4	5
11	H2	4
12	H3	4
13	H5	3
14	H10	21
15	J9	15
16	K7	13

Key number 3 is the background colour, ochre (C6). Ochre is also used in the design.

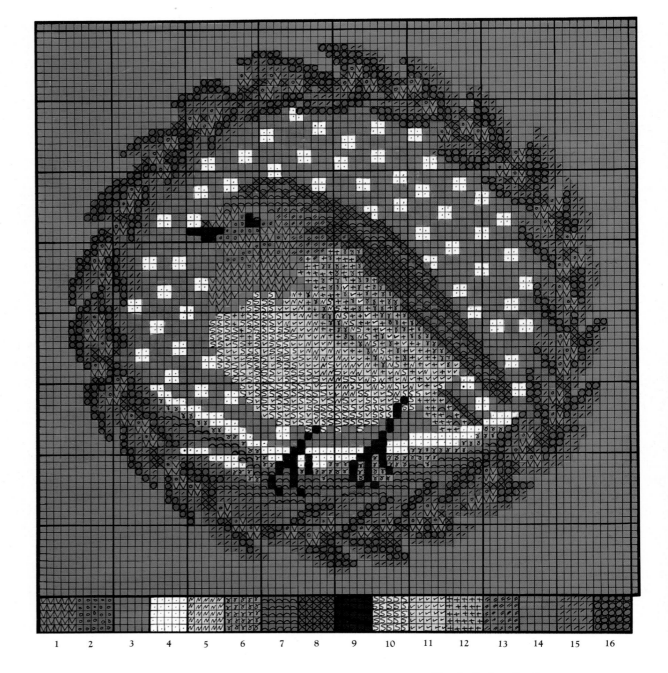

1 2 3 4 5 6 7 8 9 10 11 12 13 14 15 16

A Christmas Robin Design

The robin on this chart is perched on a branch in the falling snow, he is set in the centre of a wreath of holly leaves and berries. Made into a pincushion or small picture, this robin would make a charming Christmas greeting card or present.

"Little Robin-Redbreast
To the window comes,
Seeking warmth and shelter,
Asking us for crumbs.

Shall we not remember
All outside our door,
Whom the chill December
Finds hungry, sad and poor."

From a Victorian Christmas card.

WINTER

The Cyclamen

They are terribly white:
There is snow on the ground,
And a moon on the snow at night;
The sky is cut by the winter light;
Yet I, who have all these things
in ken,
Am struck to the heart by the
chiselled white
Of this handful of cyclamen.

"Cyclamens", Michael Field (1893)

To most people, cyclamens are pretty flowering plants that grow in pots and bring colour and freshness into the house through the late autumn and early winter. Lately they seem to come in two distinct sizes, small and delicate with dainty butterfly flowers or big, blowsy and magnificent with handsome fleshy flowers which are sometimes further elaborated by speckles, frills and ruffles. Both sizes are delightful and difficult to resist.

The potted cyclamen is the tender *Cyclamen persicum*, the large varieties being grouped under the name *C. giganteum*. In her book, *Gardens of Delight*, Eleanor Sinclair Rohde gives a paragraph of very sensible advice on how to treat them.

"Cyclamen when flowering should not stand in the sun. They have to be watered carefully so that no water touches the bulbs. Any fading leaves or flowers should be removed immediately. They should not, however, be cut but picked off with a quick twitch that brings them away from the base of the stalk. If part of the stalk were left it would only bleed and injure the bulb. Picking the flowers ensures a longer flowering period, but naturally everyone loves to see a pot massed with blooms. When they have finished flowering they should be watered less and less and given as much sun and air as possible. When quite dry the corms should be shaken free of soil and put on a tray of sand to be given all the sun-baking possible. Some growers prefer to lay the pots on their sides in a frame in May and leave them till July."

To our ancestors, cyclamens meant *Cyclamen hederifolium* or Sowbread, so-called because pigs love to eat the corms. Powdered sowbread corms could be bought in apothecaries' shops and were used to ease the pangs and process of childbirth. As a remedy it was so effective that it gave rise to the fear that it was unwise for "woemen with chylde' to ever walk over the root for fear of having a miscarriage."

Made into "trochisches, or little flat cakes", cyclamen corms were "reported to be a good amorous medicine to make one in love; if it be inwardly taken." (Gerard) Alternatively, powdered roots stuffed up the nose were a cure for hair loss. "In case that a man's hair fall off, take this same wort, and put it into the nostrils." In the language of flowers, the cyclamen means goodbye and to dream of a cyclamen is a prediction of disaster, so be warned.

Hardy Cyclamen

The small, hardy varieties of cyclamen were not widely grown in flower gardens until comparatively recently. They are very long-lived plants that can survive for more than a century. The corms can grow to the size of a large dinner plate and a seventy-year-old example presented to the Floral Committee of the Royal Horticultural Society towards the end of the nineteenth century sported at least 500 flowers and a corm the size of a baby's head.

If several species of cyclamen are grown in a garden, then cyclamen flowers may be had for most of the year. *Cyclamen hederifolium* or Sowbread, sometimes called *Cyclamen neopolitanum* needs to be planted on the surface of the earth as do most varieties of hardy cyclamen. This species is thought to be Britain's only native cyclamen and flowers from mid-summer to autumn. It was grown in the knot gardens of the Elizabethans and it bears the most highly scented of all cyclamen flowers. *C. hederifolium* grows in shade and its heart-shaped leaves are attractively marbled with white.

Cyclamen purpurescens also flowers from early summer to autumn with its leaves continuing to

---

OVERLEAF: *Potted cyclamens bring freshness into the house in late autumn when the garden is dying back and the leaves falling. The woolwork cyclamens in this picture have been worked against three different backgrounds: cream (F3), black (G11) and pale green (J2).*

1   2   3   4   5   6   7   8   9   10   11   12   13   14   15   16   17

Wool colours and quantities

The quantities listed below are the numbers of yards of Elizabeth Bradley Wool needed to work a piece 160 stitches by 160 stitches on 10 mesh interlock canvas using cross stitch.

Colours used:
17 plus 1 background colour.

The background colour of the piece shown in the carpet on page 101 is pale green (J2), the background colours of the pieces shown on pages 148-9 are cream (F3) and black (G11).

Number on Chart key	Elizabeth Bradley Wool colour	Quantity (yards)
1	A1	46
2	N5	42
3	A6	5
4	A10	20
5	A11	17
6	I6	3
7	K3	44
8	I7	12
9	J1	10
10	K2	19
11	K5	25
12	K6	21
13	K9	17
14	K10	12
15	K11	18
16	N6	23
17	A8	5

Background quantity for a piece measuring 160 stitches by 160 stitches: 210 yards.

flourish well into the following late spring. *Cyclamen cilicicum* has unusual twisted petals and blooms from early to late autumn, while *Cyclamen coum* is in flower from early winter to early spring. *Cyclamen repandum* is a mountain species and very free flowering when planted in a sheltered part of the garden, it flowers from mid- to late spring. Early summer alone is without its cyclamen.

The Cyclamen Chart

The cyclamen in this design is *Cyclamen persicum* which can be grown in sheltered spots in the garden. The heart-shaped leaves are marbled with silver and the petals of the flowers are coloured various shades of pink. The cyclamen on the chart has flowers of a shade of cold lilac-pink that is characteristic of many cyclamens.

Less hardy varieties of *Cyclamen persicum* with larger flowers come in many different colours from mauve to bright pink and red. A deep carmine and pure white have recently been developed. The pattern of the marbling on their leaves varies considerably and some of them have scented flowers. The large tender varieties of the species are normally grown as pot plants and listed under the name Giganteum. Ruffled hybrids have ruffled and fringed flowers in shades of pink, red and lilac. C. *persicum* "Grandia" has huge outspread salmon pink blooms, while the flowers of C. *persicum* "Silberstrahl" are a clear carmine laced with narrow white margins.

If you would prefer your stitched cyclamens to be a colour other than lilac-pink, then work them in three shades of whichever colour it is that you prefer. The colours on the wool list that need to be changed are numbers 1, 2 and 16.

For white cyclamen use F1, F2 and F3.

For bright pink cyclamen use A3, A4 and A5.

For red cyclamen use B11, A6 and A8 (Colours 3 and 17 will also need to be changed to N8 and N4 in this red cyclamen).

For lilac cyclamen use N5, N6 and N7.

Materials and Methods

Woolwork is normally worked on special machine-woven canvas available in a variety of colours and sizes. This canvas is described or measured by the number of mesh per inch (a mesh being the intersection where two threads cross). Ten mesh canvas has ten threads and ten holes per inch.

Interlock canvas was developed comparatively recently as a variation on the older and more conventional, single threaded, mono canvas or double threaded, Penelope canvas. On these canvases, the horizontal (weft) threads pass under and over the vertical (warp) threads as is normal on most woven fabrics. On interlock canvas, the horizontal threads actually pass through the vertical threads where they intersect, creating a firm, immovable grid. Interlock is a particularly simple and pleasant sort of canvas to use, it is especially suitable for beginners because an excellent quality of work can be achieved with very little experience.

All the woolwork designs in this book were worked on the type of canvas known as interlock. A specially strong, soft and supple brand of 10 mesh interlock canvas has been made especially for Elizabeth Bradley Designs, it is available in white only and has a width of one metre. It has a blue thread running through the selvedge and is known as Blue Line Canvas.

All the pieces in this book have been worked in full cross stitch. Ten mesh interlock canvas is the perfect size for cross stitch when it is worked with modern 4-ply tapestry wool. If half-cross stitch or tent stitch is used instead, a canvas with smaller holes, such as 12 mesh, would be a better size. White canvas threads tend to show through the stitches if 10 mesh is used.

Whatever canvas is chosen to work upon, sufficient should always be bought to allow at least a 3-in (7.5-cm) margin around the finished area of woolwork. Before starting to stitch, many people bind the edges of their canvas with masking tape to stop them unravelling. This procedure, though not strictly necessary with interlock canvas because it does not fray, is advisable in order to protect clothes and to stop the wool snagging on the cut edges of the canvas.

Woolwork should always be stitched with the selvedge running up the side of the piece being worked because the shape of the completed piece of woolwork will then be squarer. If a piece is worked with the selvedge running along the top or bottom, then the shape tends to become rather elongated. This point is especially important to remember if the finished piece is destined to be part of a carpet.

Linen for Samplers

Introducing each seasonal section of this book is a design which can either be worked as a piece of woolwork or as a sampler. All four samplers have been worked on a natural, unbleached, linen fabric known as scrim. Many period samplers were worked on very similar fabrics especially in the late eighteenth and early nineteenth centuries. The use of a natural linen is traditional and imparts a certain antique style to a modern sampler.

Scrim can often be obtained from good hardware shops where squares of it are sold as cloths for polishing glasses and it can also be bought from needlework shops. Such unbleached natural linens can be obtained in various widths and mesh sizes. The linen used for the four samplers in this book is 100% linen scrim, 91cms wide which has approximately 20 threads to the inch. It is available from branches of John Lewis, Stock number F 104 27184.

Sampler Threads

Samplers are traditionally worked in cross stitch. For ease of working, each stitch should be worked over two threads of the linen. Antique samplers were generally worked with lustrous, pure, floss silk or fine crewel wool but many modern ones, including the four seasonal samplers in this book, are worked with perle cotton. This six-stranded, slightly glossy thread comes in a good range of colours, it is easy to use and is much more readily available than pure silk. For ease of use and to further resemble period sampler silk, each thread of six strands should be divided into two threads of three strands.

Wool

All the designs in this book have been worked with Elizabeth Bradley 4-ply Wool. This range of wools contains 154 colours. Some of the wools are brightly coloured but most are slightly muted shades so that the resulting work has a rich and antique look – not too faded, but not garish either. Since most traditional furnishing fabrics use a similar range of colours, needlework using these wools will fit into many different rooms. If brighter colours than those suggested are required, then substitute a more brilliant shade for each muted one. The Elizabeth Bradley Woolbook, containing samples of all the wools organized on to 14 detachable cards, is invaluable for this purpose. A conversion chart for other brands of wool can be found on pages 161-2.

Wool Quantities

The wool quantities given in this book are for the number of yards of Elizabeth Bradley 4-ply Wool that would be needed to sew a design if cross stitch were used and if the work was done on 10 mesh, interlock canvas. These quantities should be approximately halved if either half cross stitch or tent stitch is used instead.

Most of the designs in this book are new and in some cases only one prototype of each design was worked. Consequently, the wool quantities given with each chart are only approximate. The quantities of wool used by different stitchers can vary enormously, especially in more complicated designs. When the wool quantities for an Elizabeth Bradley Kit are calculated, an extra 30% of wool is added to the average of the amounts used to make the various prototypes (at least six prototypes are usually made), this allows for mistakes and unusual ways of working. The wool quantities given in this book also include an extra 30% added to the wool that was used to make the prototype or prototypes, and because of this you may find that the wool quantities err on the side of generosity.

Buying Wool

Elizabeth Bradley Wool is wound on to cards of two sizes. The large card contains 30 yards of wool and the small, 10 yards. The lengths of wool that are in the skeins and hanks of other manufacturers are indicated in the conversion chart on pages 161-2. Care should be taken not to mix wool of different types as the thickness and degree of twist of one brand of wool can vary considerably from another. Using several together can result in an unevenly textured piece of work.

The colour of a wool may vary slightly between dye lots although the differences are minimal these days and will only occasionally cause problems. A slight difference in the shade of a wool can result in a shadowy line across an area of background and so if a large area is being worked it may be worthwhile buying all the necessary wool in one batch.

The Stitch

All the designs in this book have been worked in cross stitch. Finished pieces worked in this stitch are thicker than those made with tent stitch and so they tend to be more hard wearing. As a stitch, cross stitch is easy to work and as each individual cross forms its own small square the pattern looks very distinct. Pieces worked in cross stitch do not become distorted as each stitch pulls first to the right and then to the left leaving the finished needlework square. For this reason, it is unnecessary to use a frame to preserve the shape of a piece of woolwork, instead the canvas can be stitched while held in the hand and just rolled up loosely as the work progresses. I find working without a frame much more pleasant and convenient. It is also quicker, because when the canvas is not stretched on a frame the stitches can be formed with the hand holding the needle working entirely on the front of the canvas. On a frame it is necessary to stab the needle backwards and forwards through the canvas each time a stitch is worked: a far more tiring way to work.

There are a number of ways of working cross stitch. The particular version shown in the diagrams overleaf is one that is often found on pieces of original, Victorian woolwork, I consider it the best method and always use it myself. It is a very easy and satisfactory stitch to work although it is somewhat extravagant with wool. The wool quantities that are given with each chart in this book allow for the use of this cross stitch worked on 10 mesh interlock canvas.

The use of cross stitch is essential when making carpets because the finished piece needs to be square and remain square. Carpets worked in tent stitch would almost certainly require extensive

Cross Stitch

*To start – leave the knot on the surface
– the wool, between the knot and the
first stitch, can be worked over to anchor
it and the knot cut off later.*

1. *Pass the needle under one thread of
canvas.*

2. *Complete the stitch and then pass the
needle under two threads of canvas.*

3. *Repeat the first step, passing the
needle under one thread of canvas.*

4. *Once again pass the needle under two
threads of canvas. The needle moves
horizontally at all times.*

*Cross stitch should always be worked so
that the second of the two short stitches
of the cross all lie in the same direction.*

*Right-handed stitchers work from right to
left. Left-handed stitchers turn the
diagrams upside down and work from left
to right.*

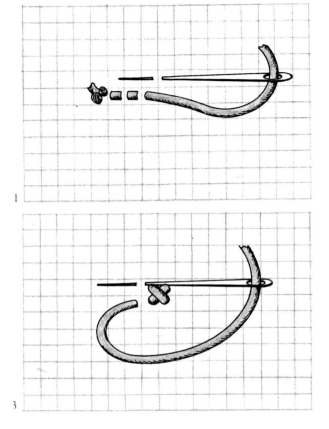

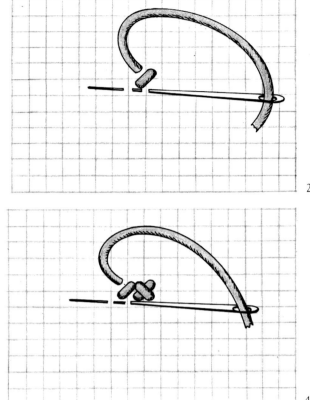

stretching and re-shaping and however carefully
this is done they always tend to creep back to being
diamond- or parallelogram-shaped – especially if
they become damp.

The Appearance of the Finished Work

The appearance of a piece of finished woolwork
depends on various factors. One of these is the
smoothness and regularity with which the work is
done. If the lengths of wool can be persuaded to
pass through the canvas without jagging, twisting
or jerking then the stitches will be much more
even and the look of the finished piece smoother
and more lustrous. Practice and experience help to
achieve an easy and relaxed working style. The
length of the strand of wool used in the needle is
also important. Long lengths of thread twist more
than shorter ones and can become thin and frayed
by the time the end has been reached. Approximately 30 ins (75 cms) of thread seems to be a good
practical length.

Another factor that affects appearance is the
direction in which the lengths of wool are used.

Wool has a right and a wrong way. If a length of
wool is pulled gently between the fingers or lips
then one direction should feel slightly smoother
than the other. Work should always be done with
the wool passing through the canvas in this direction, it will behave much better. If a length of
thread is being troublesome, try turning it around.

The quality of a finished piece can also be
affected by the tension of the stitches – the term
tension means how tightly each stitch is pulled.
Stitches should not be pulled too tightly or the
wool becomes stretched and thin, nor should they
be so slack as to form loops. The finished piece will
be smoother and even slightly larger in size if the
tension is kept quite loose. Tugging each stitch
tightly causes the piece of work to become puckered and may actually make it slightly smaller in
area. Ideally, the same tension should be used
throughout a piece. The ability to achieve this uniformity comes with practice as does an easy and
personal rhythm of stitching.

Pieces of needlework that are obviously well
executed tend to have very neat and tidy backs. To
help achieve this, ends of wool should be cut off

close to the back of the work and long loops stretching from one group of stitches to another should be avoided. If long ends and loops of more than ½in (1.25cms) are left at the back of a piece they become caught up with other stitches and the work can become terribly thick and matted.

Starting and Finishing

To begin stitching, tie a large knot in the end of the wool. Leave the knot on the front of the work about 1in (2.5cm) in front of where the stitches will start. The first few stitches will then hold the wool in place at the back of the work and the knot can be snipped off when it is reached.

To finish off, take the end of the length of wool to the back of the work and thread it through between six and ten stitches before being cut off. Take care to finish off each strand of wool properly – if only short ends of wool are anchored down when starting and finishing they can work loose very easily and make constant repairs necessary.

Correcting Mistakes

It is easy, especially when tired, to make small mistakes when following a chart. Most of these mistakes can be put right quite easily by either undoing a few stitches and re-working them or by adapting that part of the pattern slightly so that the mistake merges in with the rest of the design.

If an area of stitches does need to be undone, do so with great care. Snip through each stitch with a small, pointed pair of scissors and pull out the cut ends. When the section is re-worked, anchor down any stray ends of wool with the new stitches.

If a thread of the canvas gets cut by mistake it is possible to repair it by cutting a small square of canvas from the side of the work and tacking it behind the damaged area, matching the holes exactly. The new stitches can then be worked through both the main canvas and the patch and a practically invisible mend achieved.

Working from a Chart

Contrary to what many people think, working from a chart is both straightforward and surprisingly easy once the eye has grown used to following the squared pattern. Each square on the chart represents one stitch, and each stitch is worked over an intersection of a horizontal and a vertical thread of canvas. It is the threads of the canvas that should be counted, not the holes as one might think – hence the name counted thread work.

Reading a chart becomes quite simple once this principle has been established and all that is then required is careful counting. Each square has been painted in a shade that is as similar as possible to that of the wool that will be used to stitch it. Some of the wool colours used in a design are very similar and so symbols have been added where necessary to help avoid confusion.

Working Instructions

Where to start sewing is, to a certain extent, a matter of personal preference as is the way in which the design is worked.

Some people start in the centre of a new project, work the picture part of a design first and then fill in the background later; others start at the top and then proceed downwards. Personally, I like to start at the bottom of a piece and work upwards because I find the stitch easier to work in this way. I also like to see the pattern growing upwards from the bottom of the piece rather than downwards from the top. I tend to work the pictorial part of the design when I am feeling reasonably fresh and the background in the evening when I am tired or when I am chatting or watching television. Some of the colours used in my designs are very similar and the small differences between them can be difficult to see in bad or artificial light, so it is best to work these sections in daylight when the difference between the colours shows up more clearly. If working in daylight is not possible, then a daylight bulb is a good substitute.

Each row of stitches, whether long or short, should be worked from right to left. If the row is longer than seven or eight stitches it should be finished off at the far end and the next row started afresh. If the gap between the end of one row of stitches and the beginning of the next is less than seven or eight stitches then a loop can be left between them. Longer loops tend to get caught up and pulled tight by other stitches and this can cause the piece to become puckered and thick. Sometimes a colour is dotted about in small areas all over the design, a stitch here, two there and so on. It is tempting to loop from one area to another but this is bad practice unless the dots or small areas of colour are very close together.

When working the background, start at the right-hand side (or left-hand side if you are left handed) of the canvas and work all the way across to the other side. Finish off at the end of each row and start again on the right using the rest of the wool left in the needle. If each row of the background is started with a new length of wool in the needle, all the lengths will finish at approximately the same place. This will cause vertical and rather unsightly lines at intervals across the width of the finished background area.

Many needleworkers are absolute perfectionists. They produce magnificent work in which each stitch exactly mirrors an equivalent square on the chart, the back of such work often being as exquisite as the front. Most of us start out with this ideal in mind but fall down in the actual practice; on the whole we are content to have a completed piece of work which looks good even if it does contain a few inconsistencies. The group of needleworkers who are likely to have the most problems are those beginners who are also absolute perfectionists, for them there is no pleasure in producing work that is not totally accurate and yet their lack of experience makes this difficult. I can only suggest that they tackle simple projects until their expertise catches up with their aspirations.

Finishing

When finished, a piece of needlework should be pressed on its reverse side through a damp cloth or with a steam iron. If the finished piece is at all out of shape, stretch or block it. To do this, dampen it and stretch it into shape. Then pin the piece out to dry by fixing it down with carpet tacks or drawing pins on to a board.

Cleaning

For the purposes of cleaning, it is helpful to regard woolwork as a type of thick woollen upholstery fabric which can be washed but only if absolutely necessary and with great care, using a gentle soap powder and warm water. On the whole, it is much safer to have a finished piece dry cleaned, especially if it has already been made up into a cushion. The colours of modern tapestry wool are fast and do not run but a cushion can become puckered if the woolwork and its backing shrink to different degrees.

If a piece of woolwork has been used as a cover for an upholstered stool or chair, dry cleaning is impossible. In this case, just vacuum clean the surface of the stool or chair to remove any dust or loose dirt particles, and then sponge the needlework with an upholstery foam. Wool is protected from dirt by its own natural oils but extra protection can be given by spraying a freshly completed piece with a protective fluid, such as Scotchguard.

Antique woolwork should never be washed by an amateur as many of the colours would run and the canvas threads will have been weakened by age. Water would soften these fibres further and might even cause them to disintegrate completely. If an antique piece needs serious cleaning, it is advisable to leave the job to a professional textile restorer.

Upholstered Furniture

Pieces of woolwork make excellent covers for most types of upholstered furniture. Stools and chairs are the items most usually covered but the ambitious could try covering armchairs or ottomans.

Before a new needlework cover is attached to a piece of furniture it is advisable to have the upholstery overhauled. It is well worth having this done professionally and by traditional methods because then the piece, with its new needlework cover, should last for many years without further restoration or repair.

Many classic pieces of furniture are now reproduced and their manufacturers or stockists should be able to provide templates for their covers. If such a template is not available, the best way to determine the shape and size of a prospective chair or stool cover is to remove its original cover and use it as a pattern for the replacement. If this is not possible, then all that can be done is to measure the dimensions of the seat and draw out the approximate shape on the canvas, leaving a generous margin around the edge in case of error.

Cushions

The majority of woolwork pieces stitched today are made into cushions. Backing materials suitable for such cushions are cotton velvet, watered silk, ottoman cloth, linen or fine wool, all of which are traditional for this purpose. Most cushions are fitted with a zip which is usually inserted along the bottom or across the back. Many antique cushions were embellished with a cord sewn around the edge and a tassel at each corner. The cord and tassels should be sewn on by hand after the cushion has been made and a wide range of attractive cord and tassels are now available from department stores and specialist shops.

Cord unravels very quickly if the ends are left free and so they should be bound with thread or a small piece of sticky tape at all times. The cord should be attached by hand, stitching it all the way round using button thread and a curved needle. The cord should not be pulled tight as it is being sewn on, instead it should lie easy and unstretched against the edges of the cushion.

To start, poke one end of the cord into a small gap made in the seam and sew it in place, continue sewing right round the cushion and back to the starting point. The other end of the cord should then be pushed in next to the first and the two firmly stitched in place to make as invisible a join as possible. The tassels can be attached as each corner is reached, each tassel has a loop on top and the cord should be pushed through this loop to secure the tassel.

An alternative trim would be piping made from silk fabric cut on the cross and wrapped around a length of piping cord. A small piece of needlework can be extended by using it as the centrepiece of a fabric frame made from strips of material with their corners mitred.

Framing

Pieces of Victorian woolwork were often displayed framed on the wall rather than as cushions. Mellow, golden, maple mouldings were by far the most popular type of frame in the nineteenth century and modern maple framing is still widely used around needlework pictures and samplers today. Victorian pictures were normally glazed to protect them against the soot and tar from coal fires but with present-day centrally-heated houses this is no longer necessary and so framed woolwork is often left unglazed.

Before a piece of woolwork can be framed, it is essential to stretch it. In the past, the work would have been tacked to a specially-made wooden stretcher before being placed in the frame. Today, it is more usual to stretch it over a piece of hardboard or card before framing.

The hardboard should be slightly smaller than the frame. Place the needlework face downwards on a table and lay the hardboard on top. Using thin string or strong twine, lace the top and bottom edges together, gradually pulling the string tighter and tighter. This should be done gently because if the string or twine is jerked tight suddenly it might break and could even tear the canvas; time is needed for the canvas to stretch to its fullest extent. When laced tight enough, repeat the process with the lacing running from one side of the piece to the other.

The picture in its frame should be backed with card or mounting board cut to the right shape. This can then be fastened down with panel pins or metal triangles from a mounting gun. Finally, the join between card and frame should be covered with gummed paper tape. It is always interesting to see pictures that have been signed and dated, it adds interest and such extra details are a kindness to antique dealers of the future who will be very pleased to have their pieces dated for them.

Information

ELIZABETH BRADLEY NEEDLEWORK KITS

The Lily, The Pansy and The Cyclamen designs featured in this book are available as kits from Elizabeth Bradley Designs Limited, their distributors, and from leading stores and needlework stockists. These kits are numbered 36, 39 and 40 respectively in The Botanical Garden series.

Each kit contains:
- Canvas (10 mesh interlock) printed with the design in colour.
- A full-size colour chart to help work the design accurately.
- Sufficient wool to work the design in a full cross stitch.
- Comprehensive instructions and a history leaflet.
- Background wool and a background wool changing leaflet.
- A woolcard with samples of all the wools used for the design and the seven background colours.
- Two needles.

All these components are enclosed in an attractive box which makes the kits highly suitable as gifts.

The following items and services are also available from Elizabeth Bradley Designs Limited:

- An illustrated 44-page colour catalogue.
- Elizabeth Bradley 4-ply tapestry wool, wound on to cards of two sizes: Large – 30 yards, and Small – 10 yards.
- A Woolfax containing samples of the full range of the Elizabeth Bradley wools.
- Elizabeth Bradley Blue Line Canvas: 10 mesh interlock canvas, one metre wide, available by the metre (Minimum order – 1 metre).
- Cord, tassels and brass bell pull ends.
- The Ribbon and Bow Carpet Border Kit available in red, blue or green.
- The book *Decorative Victorian Needlework* by Elizabeth Bradley.
- A cushion-making service.
- A framing service.

The full range of Elizabeth Bradley Needlework Kits is as follows:

The Victorian Animal Series
(16×16ins [40×40cms])
1 The Cream Cat
2 The King Charles Spaniel
3 The Cockerel
4 The Mother Hen
5 The Parrot
6 The Three Birds
7 Toby the Pug
8 The Contented Cat
9 The Spotted Dog
10 The Squirrel
11 The Lion
12 The Elephant

The Four Seasons
Victorian Flower Series
(16×16ins [40×40cms])
13 Spring
14 Summer
15 Autumn
16 Winter

A Flowered Victorian Bell Pull
(46×6ins [115×15cms])

The Fruits of the Earth Series
(16×16ins [40×40cms])
17 Strawberries
18 A Bowl of Fruit
19 Vegetables
20 A Wreath of Herbs

The Beasts of the Field Series
(13.3×20.3ins [33.25×50.75cms])
21 The Gloucester Old Spot Sow
   with her Piglets
22 The Shorthorn Ox
23 The Suffolk Punch with a Hound
24 Two Fat Suffolk Lambs

Decorative Victorian Needlework
(16×16ins [40×40cms])
25 A Wreath of Roses
26 Repeating Roses
27 A Posy of Violets
28 Patchwork Pieces

The Botanical Garden
(16×16ins [40×40cms])
29 The Crocus
30 The Daffodil
31 The Tulip
32 The Auricula
33 The Pink
34 The Rose
35 The Daisy
36 The Lily
37 The Hollyhock
38 The Hydrangea
39 The Pansy
40 The Cyclamen

ELIZABETH BRADLEY DISTRIBUTORS

AUSTRALIA

Lauren Exclusives
53 William Edward Street, Longueville
New South Wales 2066
Australia
Tel: (2) 427 51 47 Fax: (2) 602 86 87
Contact: Kim Annan

BELGIUM

CHC International
Spoorwegstraat 7, 1610 Ruisbroek
Belgium
Tel: (2) 237 822 88 Fax: (2) 237 832 79
Contact: Claudine Dierckx

CANADA

SR Kertzer Ltd
105 A Winges Road, Woodbridge
Ontario
Canada
LAL 6C2
Toll No: 1 (800) 263 2354
Tel: (416) 856 3447 Fax: (416) 856 5585
Contact: Heather Patterson

FINLAND

Hannisign Oy
Jarvihaantie 5, 01800 Klakkula
Finland
Tel: (08) 79 38 43 Fax: (08) 79 84 36
Contact: Hanni Akrenius

FRANCE

Voisine
12 rue de L'Eglise, 92200 Neuilly sur Seine
Paris
France
Tel: (1) 46 37 54 60 Fax: (1) 46 24 23 28
Contact: Christine Combermarle

GERMANY

Offerta Versand
Bruneckerstrasse 2A, D6080,
Gross Gerau
Germany
Tel: (6) 1 52 56 964 Fax: (6) 1 52 53 705
Contact: Sigurd Plaumann

ICELAND

Troels Bendsten & Co
PO Box 334, 15 121 Reykjavik
Iceland
Tel: (01) 627557 Fax: (01) 627550
Contact: Troels Bendsten

ITALY

D & C Spa
Divisione Sybilla
Via Nannetti 1, 40069 Zola Predosa
Bologna
Italy
Tel: (51) 61 72 88 or (51) 75 88 55
Fax: (51) 75 91 53
Contact: Marina Cariona

JAPAN

Sangei Imports Ltd
2-64 Hirakata, Fukuju-cho
Hashima-shi, Gifu, 501-62, Japan
Tel: 81 (583) 98 5144
Fax: 81 (583) 98 5132
Contact: Mikio Yamada

SPAIN

Muelledos SL
Juan Bravo 26, 28006 Madrid
Spain
Tel: (1) 435 47 76 Fax: (1) 571 32 72
Contact: Ana Cardenal

SWEDEN

Country House
Jungmansgatan 37, 41311 Goteburg
Sweden
Tel: (31) 12 63 32 Fax: (31) 12 63 32
Contact: Gunilla Berglie

SWITZERLAND

Arcalaine
8 Rue de Vieux College, 1204 Geneva
Switzerland
Tel: (2) 23 11 74 02 Fax: (2) 23 12 28 48
Contact: Claude Poncet

USA

Potpourri Etc
PO Box 78, Redondo Beach
California 90277
Toll free number: (800) 548 6022
Tel: (310) 322 8512 Fax: (310) 322 8512
Contact: Jean Dittrich

The full range of kits, accessories and services
is available direct from Elizabeth Bradley
Designs Limited as follows:

Elizabeth Bradley Designs Limited
1 West End, Beaumaris
Anglesey
N Wales
LL58 8BD
Tel: (0248) 811055 Fax: (0248) 811118

US customers may order from:
Elizabeth Bradley Inc
PO Box 66599
Chicago AMF
Illinois 60666
Toll Free Number: 1 (800) 635 0974

OVERLEAF: *A carpet made from the 12 kits from the Botanical Garden Series edged with the Ribbon*
and Bow Border worked in green wools. The charts for The Lily, The Pansy and The Cyclamen can
be found on pages 58, 113 and 150.

CONVERSION CHART

WOOL NUMBERS-EQUIVALENT COLOURS

Number in brackets = nearest available equivalent colour

Elizabeth Bradley	Anchor	DMC	Appleton	Elizabeth Bradley	Anchor	DMC	Appleton
A1	8362	7120	141	E1	9402	7724	761
A2	8344	7950	221	E2	9424	7423	901
A3	8366	7194	222	E3	9386	(7455)	763
A4	8346	7354	223	E4	9404	7494	902
A5	(8400)	7196	224	E5	9406	7846	903
A6	(8402)	7147	226	E6	8064	7508	697
A7	9602	7449	127	E7	8104	7845	904
A8	8424	7219	759	E8	(9450)	7457	766
A9	9636	7463	122	E9	9494	7700	767
A10	9638	7465	302	E10	9452	7459	304
A11	9600	7165	125	E11	9496	7479	305
B1	9592	7451	702	F1	8004	blanc	991
B2	9594	7543	202	F2	8006	blanc	992
B3	9596	7164	203	F3	8034	ecru	882
B4	9598	7123	204	F4	(9052)	7500	988
B5	8326	7124	205	F5	9654	7491	984
B6	8328	7146	206	F6	9324	7523	951
B7	8312	7178	207	F7	9328	7511	952
B8	8264	7447	208	F8	(9388)	7524	953
B9	8196	7850	865	F9	9408	7514	914
B10	8238	7920	866	F10	(9394)	7488	955
B11	8204	7108	504	F11	9396	7489	916
C1	9322	7501	691	G1	9482	7520	981
C2	8038	7493	692	G2	9364	7519	982
C3	8040	7503	693	G3	9366	(7462)	183
C4	8042	(7725)	473	G4	9368	(7465)	986
C5	8060	7505	695	G5	9392	(7518)	184
C6	8062	7781	696	G6	(9662)	(7499)	186
C7	8140	7767	475	G7	9642	7467	187
C8	(8156)	7444	476	G8	(9644)	7468	582
C9	9532	7173	861	G9	9648	7515	584
C10	(8234)	7875	863	G10	9666	7419	588
C11	9538	7446	479	G11	9800	7309	993
D1	8012	7905	841	H1	9052	7390	971
D2	8014	7470	331	H2	(9054)	7331	972
D3	8056	7472	471	H3	(9054)	(7415)	973
D4	8016	7727	842	H4	(9068)	(7415)	974
D5	8018	7473	843	H5	(9372)	7416	976
D6	8020	7484	311	H6	9772	7270	989
D7	9284	7785	844	H7	9774	7282	962
D8	9286	7474	312	H8	9790	7618	963
D9	9288	7485	313	H9	9776	7273	964
D10	9290	7487	314	H10	9794	7620	965
D11	9292	7490	315	H11	9764	(7713)	967

Elizabeth Bradley	Anchor	DMC	Appleton	Elizabeth Bradley	Anchor	DMC	Appleton
I1	9196	7583	252	L1	8874	7322	521
I2	9306	7353	241	L2	8896	7692	152
I3	(9308)	7582	332	L3	8898	7323	154
I4	9214	7363	242	L4	8878	7327	155
I5	9260	7426	343	L5	8882	7326	156
I6	(9174)	7362	344	L6	8884	7701	158
I7	9216	7364	345	L7	8906	7429	159
I8	9330	7355	334	L8	8894	7292	921
I9	9218	(7355)	244	L9	(8736)	7293	922
I10	9312	7391	336	L10	8738	7592	324
I11	9314	7425	348	L11	8740	7297	928
J1	9058	7400	351	M1	8820	7813	565
J2	9256	(7373)	352	M2	8822	7650	566
J3	(9096)	(7382)	353	M3	8792	7306	853
J4	(9098)	7384	354	M4	8812	7928	876
J5	(9262)	7376	355	M5	8714	(7715)	886
J6	9202	(7364)	255	M6	(8604)	(7241)	741
J7	9204	(7367)	546	M7	8626	7799	742
J8	9206	7367	357	M8	8638	7308	852
J9	9208	7379	548	M9	8742	7299	929
J10	9166	7547	544	M10	8594	7245	105
J11	9168	7988	545	M11	(8596)	(7791)	106
K1	8892	7321	151	N1	9676	7232	931
K2	9064	7333	291	N2	(9680)	7234	932
K3	9074	7392	292	N3	(9682)	7236	933
K4	9076	7394	293	N4	9684	7238	934
K5	9078	7396	294	N5	8504	7213	711
K6	9080	7890	297	N6	8506	7223	712
K7	9082	7347	298	N7	8508	7226	713
K8	(8874)	7704	641	N8	8510	7115	715
K9	(8876)	7335	642	N9	8546	7896	603
K10	(8880)	7702	644	N10	8548	7895	605
K11	9028	7408	647	N11	8552	(7257)	606

Lengths of Different Manufacturers' Skeins and Hanks

	Skein	Hank
Elizabeth Bradley (on cards)	10yd (9.2m)	30yd (27.6m)
Anchor	10.8yd (10m)	–
DMC	8.8yds (8m)	–
Appleton	10yd (9.2m)	60yd (55m)

Bibliography

A Book of English Poetry, Chaucer to Rossetti, collected by G B Harrison (Penguin Books, 1940)

Addison, Josephine *The Illustrated Plant Lore* (Guild Publishing, 1985)

Arkell, Reginald *Green Fingers – A Present For A Good Gardener* (Herbert Jenkins Limited, 1934)

Arkell, Reginald, *Green Fingers Again – A Further Present For A Good Gardener* (Herbert Jenkins Limited, 1942)

Bank, Mirra *Anonymous Was A Woman* (St Martin's Press, New York, 1979)

Blunt, Wilfrid *The Art of Botanical Illustration* (Collins, 1950)

Brooke, Rupert *The Poetical Works of*, ed by G Keynes (Faber and Faber Ltd, 1946)

Carter, Tom *The Victorian Garden* (Bracken Books, Bestseller Publications Ltd, 1988)

Chinery, Michael *Collins Guide to the Insects of Britain and Western Europe* (Collins, London, 1986)

Clare, John *The Shepherd's Calendar* ed by E Robinson and G Summerfield (Oxford University Press, 1964)

Clarke, E and Wright, G *English Topiary Gardens* (Weidenfeld and Nicolson, 1988)

Coats, Peter *Flowers in History* (Weidenfeld and Nicolson, 1970)

Coats, Peter *Roses* (Octopus Books Limited, 1973)

Duthie, Ruth *Florists' Flowers and Societies* (Shire Publications, 1988)

Emboden, William *Narcotic Plants* (Macmillan Publishing Co Inc, New York, 1979)

Ewart, Neil *The Lore of Flowers* (Blandford Press, 1982)

Farrar, Elizabeth *Pansies, Violas and Sweet Violets* (Hurst Village Publishing, 1989)

Fawdry, Marguerite and Brown, Deborah *The Book of Samplers* (Lutterworth Press, 1980)

Fleming, Lawrence and Alan Gore *The English Garden* (Spring Books, 1979)

Friend, Rev. Hilderic *Flowers and Flower Lore, Vol I* (George Allen and Unwin Ltd)

Friend, Rev. Hilderic *Flowers and Flower Lore, Vol II* (George Allen and Unwin Ltd)

Fuller, Rodney *Pansies, Violas and Violettas – The Complete Guide* (The Crowood Press, 1990)

Gerard's Herbal – The essence thereof distilled by Marcus Woodward, from the edition of Th. Johnson (The Minerva Press, London 1971)

Genders, Roy *Collecting Antique Plants: The History and Culture of The Old Florists' Flowers* (Pelham Books, 1971)

Genders, Roy *Growing Old-Fashioned Flowers* (David & Charles, 1975)

Gordon, Lesley *Poorman's Nosegay, Flowers from a Cottage Garden* (Collins and Harvill Press, London, 1973)

Gostelow, Mary *Art of Embroidery, Great Needlework Collections of Britain and the United States* (EP Dutton, New York, 1979)

Guide to the birds of Britain and Europe (Heinzel, Fitter and Parslow, Collins)

Hager, Ben, R *The Iris – the rainbow flower* photographs by Josh Westrich (Thames and Hudson, 1989)

Hall, James *Dictionary of Subject and Symbols In Art* (John Murray, 1974)

Harrington, Caroline *A Celebration of Christmas* (Octopus Publishing Group, 1989)

Hayden, Ruth *Mrs Delaney – her life and her flowers* (Colonnade Books, 1980)

Hodges, Felice *Period Pastimes. A Practical Guide to Four Centuries of Decorative Crafts* (Weidenfeld and Nicolson, London)

Hopkins, Gerard Manley *Selected Poems* ed by J Reeves (Heinemann, 1953)

Hortus – A Gardening Journal No 22 Vol 6, 2 Summer 1992 (Hortus, Rhayader)

Hymns Old and New, ed by K Mayhew (K. Mayhew, 1977)

Jefferson-Brown, Michael *Lilies – Their Care and Cultivation* (Cassell Publishers Limited, 1990)

Kennedy-Bell, MG *The Glory of The Garden* (A & C Black Ltd, 1923)

Krutch, Joseph Wood *The Gardener's World* (GP Putnam's Sons, New York (1959)

Lack, D *The Life of the Robin* (HF & G Witherby)

Landwehr-Vogels, Josephine *Historische Kruissteekpatronen* (Zomer & Keuning Boeken BV, Ede, 1984)

Leighton, Ann *Early English Gardens in New England* (Cassell & Company Ltd, 1970)

Massingham, Betty *A Century of Gardeners* (Faber and Faber Limited, 1982

Meller, Susan and Joost Elffers *Textile Designs* (Thames and Hudson, 1991)

Muir, Frank and Jamie *A Treasury of Christmas* (Robson Books, 1981)

Phillips, Roger and Martyn Rix *Bulbs* (Pan Books Ltd, 1981)

Pimlott, JAR *The Englishman's Christmas – A Social History* (The Harvester Press, 1978)

Proctor, Molly G *Victorian Canvas Work: Berlin Wool Work* (BT Batsford Limited, 1972)

Ring, Betty *Needlework – An Historical Survey* (The Main Street Press, Pittstown, New Jersey, 1984)

Sackville-West, Vita *The Land and the Garden* ed by P Firmin (Webb & Bower, 1989)

Scourse, Nicolette *The Victorians and their Flowers* (Croom Helm, 1983)

Shakespeare, William *Complete Works* (Lewis's Ltd)

Sinclair Rohde, Eleanour *Gardens of Delight* (The Medici Society, 1934)

Sinclair Rohde, Eleanour and Parker, Eric *The Gardener's Week-End Book* (Seeley Service & Co Ltd)

Sinclair Rohde, Eleanour *The Scented Garden* (The Medici Society, 1931)

Sitwell, Sacheverell *Old Fashioned Flowers* (Country Life Limited, 1939)

Snook, Barbara *English Embroidery* (Mills & Boon Ltd, London, 1960)

Synge, Lanto *Antique Needlework* (Blandford Press, Poole, Dorset, 1982)

The Language of Flowers (Ballantyne Hanson & Co)

The Oxford Book of English Verse 1250-1918 (Oxford University Press, 1939 ed)

The Oxford Book of Light Verse (Oxford University Press, 1962 ed)

The Reader's Digest Encyclopaedia of Garden Plants and Flowers (The Reader's Digest Association Limited, London)

The Royal School of Needlework *Book of Needlework and Embroidery* (Wm Collins Sons & Co Ltd 1986)

The Week-End Book (Purnell and Sons Ltd, 1924)

Verey, Rosemary *The Garden in Winter* (Windward, 1988)

Victoria Book of Days (Hearst Books, New York)

Virgil *The Georgics* translated by CD Lewis

Words for all Seasons chosen by Malcolm Saville (Lutterworth Press, 1979)

Acknowledgments

My grateful thanks to all the needlewomen and men who stitched the prototypes for this book with such skill and patience:

Jan Bieniek for the Autumn Sampler and joining the carpet with the Nasturtium Border.

Mrs Carciero for the woolwork Autumn Sampler.

Olwen Chapple for a Sunflower and The Blackbird's Nest

Janet Davis for a pair of pansies.

Mrs Anthea Davis for the Primavera carpet which she made single handed and the Patchwork carpet, which was made virtually single handed with some help from Maurice Wells.

Diane Dewberry for Joseph Arthur's Rosebaby picture.

John Dobinson for checking charts.

Jill Evans for making cushions and small bags.

Vicki Evans for a small Poppy and a Christmas Pudding.

Mrs AG Fairhead for a tartan square and a Nasturtium bell pull.

Peter Fraser for small tartan squares and a square of Patchwork.

Sharon Granton for a Rosebaby and an alphabet.

Christine Gray for a Roses and Lace circle.

Sandy Hattenboer for a Sunflower square.

Moira Hughes for an Oak Wreath on red tartan.

Ann Jones for part of a tartan square.

Margaret Jones Evans for the woolwork version of the Spring Sampler.

Susan Jones for a Pansy.

Mrs D Kelly for Christmas Roses.

Gerrie Kostik for a Sunflower Circle and a Christmas Stocking.

Mrs G Lamb for Christmas Roses.

Edna Maskell for Roses and Lace and some tartan.

Karen Narkiewicz for making cushions.

Candice Nordhoff for the panel of two Pots of Primroses and a red tartan square.

Lynda Owen for a Nasturtium border piece and an alphabet.

Lynn Page for a Bunch of Spring Flowers, an alphabet and a Cyclamen.

Sandra L Peters for Roses and Lace.

Amanda Puryer for some blue tartan and a length of Nasturtium border.

Mrs PJ Puryer for a panel of the Sunflower Border centre, a Sunflower square, a Lily and a Primrose.

Mr C Puryer for an Iris and a length of Sunflower Border.

Pamela Quail for an Iris, an Oak Leaf Wreath and the woolwork version of the Winter Sampler.

Irene Roberts for the border around the label on the cover of the book (UK edition), a Primavera stool cover, a Bunch of Spring Flowers, the large Sunflower Border square and two corner pieces from the Nasturtium border.

Mrs K Robertson for a Lily.

Mrs Rowe for a length of Nasturtium Border.

Denise Sheridan for Poppy circles and two Christmas Puddings.

Winnie Smith for cushion making.

Mrs P Statham for a Poppy square.

Mrs Stokes for Roses and Lace, a length of Sunflower Border and two Nasturtium Border lengths.

Jenny Strom for a Roses and Lace and a piece of Patchwork.

Mairwen Strom for checking charts and for making a Primrose in a Pot, a Blackbird's Nest, a Rosebaby, an alphabet and a Christmas Pudding.

Gordon Tucker who stitched the Spring, Summer and Winter Samplers, A Nasturtium corner, some zigzag border and a Robin.

Joyce Tucker for the woolwork version of the Summer Sampler, an Iris, Christmas Roses, some small patches and two Robins.

Maurice Wells for his help with the Patchwork carpet and for making a Christmas Stocking.

Angela Williams for a small Rosebaby with blue sky.

The publishers also wish to thank the following:

Joseph Arthur Lillington for being the rosebaby on page 81 and *Thomas Jenkin Edmond Hughes* for being the boy asleep in bed on page 137.

The Rachel Kay-Shuttleworth Collection Trustees, Gawthorpe Hall, Padiham, near Burnley, Lancashire BB12 8UA who gave permission for the use of an original Berlin woolwork chart from their collection. This chart acted as the inspiration and model for the Sunflower Border chart on pages 70-1.

Tregwynt Woollen Mill, Castle Morris, Haverfordwest, Pembrokeshire SA62 5UX who supplied the checked woollen blankets in the Rosebaby picture on page 81.

Robert Young Antiques and *Rivière* at 68 Battersea Bridge Road, London SW11 who supplied the furniture and many of the props in the spring section of the book and in the photographs on pages 8-9 and 110-11.

Soulieado, 171 Fulham Road, London SW3 6JW for all the items made from their French Provençal fabric on the bed on pages 8-9 and in the suitcase on page 61.

Spice Craft, 7 Swarthmore Road, Birmingham B29 4NG for the nut wreaths and loose nuts in the autumn chapter opening picture on pages 84-5.

Bourne Farm, Halstead, Essex CO9 1LX for the pale pink rosebuds used in the wedding day picture on page 76-7.

VV Rouleaux, 201 New Kings Road, London SW6 for the ribbons shown on the shelves in the open armoire on page 43.

Global Village Crafts Ltd. Sparrow Works, Bower Hinton, Martock, Somerset TA12 6LT for the sunflower basket seen on the grass in the summer chapter opening picture on pages 48-9.

Somerset Creative Products, Brickyard Farm, Combe Lane, Wedmore, Somerset, BS28 4DZ for the Somerset trug filled with flowers and foliage on the floor in the picture on page 69.

Bleddyn Wynn Jones from Crûg Farm Nurseries, Griffiths Crossing, Near Caernarfon, Gwynedd, Wales LL55 1TU for his expert advice and the contribution of many interesting flowers and berries to the autumn and winter sampler frames, also for providing the plants in the photograph on pages 94-5.

The author and publishers have made every effort to secure permission for the poetry and prose extracts used in this book. We may have failed in a few cases to trace the copyright holder. We apologise for any apparent negligence.

Index